Sailing with God

Praying Simply

Fr. Francis Chun, S.T.L.

Sailing with God

Sailing with God

Praying Simply

Fr. Francis Chun, S.T.L.

*To Marty & Jovanna
with God's Blessings!
Fr. Chun*

Paschal Peace Press

Sailing with God

Paschal Peace Press

Cover and book designed by Tony Tarr

ISBN: 9780578412061
Library of Congress Control Number: 2018963766

1. Prayer   2. Spirituality   4. Holiness

Paschal Peace Press

With profound gratitude this book is dedicated to-

The Holy Spirit, the Spirit of Prayer and the Source of true wisdom.

A special thanks to Tony Tarr for the typesetting, for designing the cover and the entire book!

Illustrations by Tony Tarr. All rights reserved.

A big thanks to Leanne Mills (YourLadyinRED) for all her help.

Foreward

When the Catechism of the Catholic Church was given to the Church in 1994, many were delighted by the fact that the fourth and final part of the new catechism was entirely dedicated to the subject of Christian prayer. It is widely held that this emphasis of the catechism on prayer bears the personal mark of Pope St. John Paul II, who is regarded as a pope particularly devoted to the spiritual life and the practice of prayer, as exhibited by his own life.

Prayer, even the deepest forms of contemplative prayer, is not something to be left to the religious "professionals", i.e. priests and consecrated persons. It is an essential part of the life of every Christian. All of us are called to a life of prayer, from the pope all the way down to every lay man and woman engaged in the ordinary activities and duties of everyday life. But the challenge for many people is learning how to pray.

"Prayer cannot be reduced to the spontaneous outpouring of interior impulse: in order to pray, one must have the will to pray. Nor is it enough to know what the Scriptures reveal about prayer: one must also learn how to pray. Through a living transmission (Sacred Tradition) within 'the believing and praying Church,' the Holy Spirit teaches the children of God how to pray." (Catechism of the Catholic Church, 2650 – emphasis added)

Far too often the practice of prayer is regarded as something mysterious, complicated or difficult. We tend to overcomplicate what is actually the simplest of things. The only truly difficult thing about prayer is having the will to pray and the perseverance in the daily practice of prayer.

What Fr. Chun does in this very practical and easy to understand book is to make accessible to all the "how to" of prayer. The subtitle of his work says it all: Praying Simply. The practice of prayer need not be complicated. All we have to do is set our hearts on the Lord and our desire to meet him in the deep recesses of our soul.

Fr. Chun uses the simple and beautiful imagery of "Sailing with God," a very useful and practical way to enter into the dimensions of mental prayer. Drawing upon our rich Catholic spiritual tradition, along with his many years of experience as a teacher and spiritual director, he shows us how to set out on the sea of prayer, pushed along by the breath of the Holy Spirit.

It is my hope that many will pick up this simple book and learn how to pray in a way that has, up till now, seemed out of reach for some. May the reader be blessed as he or she discovers whole new horizons in their prayerful communion with our loving and merciful God. He is calling you. It is part of the universal call to holiness that is ours by virtue of our baptism. May you answer the call to prayer.

Most Reverend Alexander Sample,
Archbishop of Portland, Oregon -

Preface

After a long, serious use of this book on praying simply,
I feel like I have taken a journey with the Holy Spirit through
its words that will forever be a part of me. I will draw from
this always. Each thought, page, sentence, quote and word
has found its way into my heart. Each one a guiding post
to help me when life gets difficult. The idea of calming our
lives and knowing that God is with us with unfaltering help
and love settles my heart and soul. This book has helped
me to see through its words and through the scriptures
that life is very simple. This was a hard journey but a good
journey. It forced me to reach into the much needed love
and help of the Holy Spirit. I was able to realize first hand
of how much we are capable of if we let God direct us in
this big ocean of life.

Tony Lee Tarr

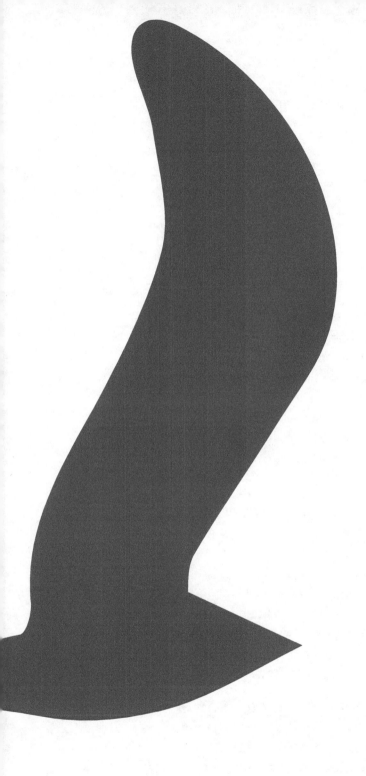

Table of Contents

Part 1

SETTING SAIL

Ⓐ My Journey with God • xxii

    a. Prelude to Prayer • 1

    b. A Sailboat • 2

    c. The Benefits of Praying • 4

    d. Simply Praying • 6

    e. The Practice of Prayer • 8

    f. The Spirit of Prayer • 10

    g. Kinds of Prayer • 12

    h. Liturgical Prayer • 14

Ⓑ Understanding Prayer • 17

    a. Questions • 18

    b. Answers • 19

    c. Basic Realities • 26

    d. Notes on Prayer • 31

    e. Having the Right Intention • 33

    f. The Healing Power of God Within Me • 36

    g. God's Healing and Help • 37

    h. Being Open to God • 38

Ⓒ My Inner Journey to God • 40

    a. My Need for Prayer • 41

    b. My Need for God • 42

    c. The Breath of Life • 43

d. The Healer Within • 44

e. Relaxing My Body for Prayer • 45

f. Calming My Inner Self for Prayer • 47

g. The Need for Inner Peace • 48

h. My Daily Contact with God • 50

Ⓓ The Commotion Within • 51

a. Why All the Commotion? • 52

b. Praying with the Commotion • 53

c. Can Emotions Block My Prayer? • 54

d. Dealing with My Emotions • 55

e. Directing the Inner Flow for Prayer • 56

Ⓔ Obstacles to Prayer • 57

a. The God of Reality • 58

b. Self-made Obstacles • 59

c. A Forgiving God • 60

d. Praying with Distractions • 61

e. God Here and Now • 64

Benefits of Prayer • 65

The Spirit of Prayer • 66

Ⓕ Resources for Reflection • 68

Consecration to the Holy Spirit • 75

Serenity Prayers • 76

Part 2
CHALLENGES

A Praying for Others • 85
    a. Toxic Grudges • 86
    b. Difficult Grudges • 87
    c. The Way of Forgiveness • 90
    d. Praying for My Foes • 91
    e. The Peace of Acceptance • 92
    f. Bonding Through Prayer • 94
    g. Prayers of Love • 96
    Abbot John Chapman – with comments • 97
    The Spirit of Freedom • 107
    The Jesus Prayer • 109
    Two Zen Monks • 112
    Father Damien of Molokai • 114
    Lectio Divina • 115
    The Sacred Liturgy as the Mystery of our Redemption • 119
    Prayer of Saint Francis • 124

B The Gifts of the
  Holy Spirit for Prayer • 126
  a. Knowledge • 127
  b. Understanding • 128
  c. Wisdom • 129
  d. Counsel • 130
  e. Fear of the Lord • 131
  f. Piety • 132
  g. Fortitude • 133

C Resources for Reflection • 134

Part 3
ARRIVING

The Heart of Prayerfulness • 158
The Prayer of Jesus for Oneness • 159

A The Radiance of God Within • 165
a. God's Peace • 166
b. God's Light • 167
c. God's Wisdom • 170
d. God's Strength • 171
e. God's Love • 172

B Radiance with God's Brightness • 173
a. Being Still • 174
b. APT Living for God • 175
c. Flowing with God • 176
d. A Channel of God's Peace • 178
e. God is Love • 179
f. God Within Me • 180
g. The Guest Within • 181
h. Come, Holy Spirit • 182
i. Receiving God's Goodness • 184

j. God's Gifts • 185
Gift 1 - God's Light • 186
Gift 2 - God's Wisdom • 187
Gift 3 - God's Strength • 188
Gift 4 - God's Love • 189
Gift 5 - God's Truth and Justice • 191
Gift 6 - God's Joy and Purity • 192
Gift 7 - God's Beauty • 193
"Lower a Bucket" - a true story • 194

Ⓒ Resources for Reflection • 196
The Spirit of Holiness • 218
An Important Parable • 219
A Parable • 220
Act of Consecration to the Holy Spirit • 222
Prayer for the Seven Gifts of the Holy Spirit • 223
Novena to the Holy Spirit (Especially for Pentecost) • 224
Conclusion • 236
Index • 238

Introduction

God is the beginning, the middle, and the goal of prayer. God invites us to union with Him in prayer, provides the help we need, and embraces us in prayer. The Holy Spirit, the Spirit of Prayer, will teach us and guide us in the journey of our prayer life.

St. Thomas Aquinas wrote: "Grace builds on nature". Because our human nature is the primary foundation of prayer, the practical psychological suggestions offered in this book will be helpful. The secondary foundation of our prayer life is the theological virtues of Faith, Hope, and Charity; that is, Faith in God, Reliance on God, and Love for God and for others.

This practical workbook will lead you on a long journey of developing a deep prayer life. Praying is simple, but the journey of prayer encounters obstacles that seem to complicate praying.

The first part introduces beginners to the practice of prayer, and guides them along the way to a deeper prayer life. Explanations and examples are provided to clarify the process of praying for a better understanding of prayer and its dynamics.

The second part will lead you to deeper ways of praying, with instruction and examples for dealing with the challenges that will arise. The long journey of a prayer life has its ups and downs, turns and twists, and sidetracks. This section will guide and help you through these challenges.

The third part will lead you through the practice of contemplative prayer. Simplifying your praying draws you into contemplation, which requires a deeper faith and greater reliance on the Holy Spirit.

The resources at the end of each part provide some of the best insights into prayer. These profound insights require serious pondering.

The ultimate goal of all prayer is to lead us to loving God with one's whole mind, whole heart, whole strength; and to love others as Christ loves them.

Part 1

SETTING SAIL

As you read,
as you learn
to pray, as you
go through life,
above you the
Holy Spirit will
always be there
to help

Holy Spirit

You

(A) My Journey with God
The Mental Preparation

a. Prelude to Prayer
b. A Sailboat
c. The Benefits of Praying
d. Simply Praying
e. The Practice of Prayer
f. The Spirit of Prayer
g. Kinds of Prayer
h. Liturgical Prayer

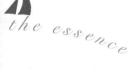

the essence of prayer is intention, not attentic

a. Prelude to Prayer

"Where can I go from your spirit?
from your presence where can I flee?
If I go up to the heavens, you are there;
If I sink to the nether world,
you are present there." Psalm 139:7-8

Because God is everywhere —
within me at the center of my soul —
I can pray anywhere, anytime.

Because God loves me and cares about me,
He will hear my every prayer.

Because I can talk, I can pray.

Because I can think, I can pray.

Because I can love, I can pray.

I will pray for others and for myself.

e essence of prayer is intention, not attention

b. A Sailboat

It's important that you pray often and regularly,
but it doesn't matter how you pray.
Prayer is union with God, being with God.

Praying is like being in a small sailboat
with God steering and the Holy Spirit blowing it along.

The following factors do not change the reality of your
praying, your being with God:
- smooth, choppy, or stormy sea;
  (your state of mind and/or emotional state)

- calm, changing, or blustery winds;
  (your situation and/or circumstances of life)

- various sea birds or creatures coming or going;
  (the distractions that come and go)

- whether you're alert or not, comfortable or not,
  fearful or not; (your physical-psychological state)

- whether you're talking to God or just being silent

*You are praying because you are with God. God
accepts you as you are, no matter your situation
or your circumstances.*

the essence of prayer is intention, not attentio

While Praying:

- Whether your state of mind or emotional state is smooth, choppy, or stormy does not matter.
- Whether your present situation or circumstances of life is calm, changing, or blustery does not matter.
- Whether few or many distractions come or go does not matter.
- Whether you're alert or drowsy, with comfort, discomfort or pain, fearful or calm does not matter

e essence of prayer is intention, not attention

c. The Benefits of Praying

A stronger faith

A deeper trust in God

Greater awareness of God's presence

Being more humble

Being more forgiving

An increase in patience and inner peace

Greater psychological/spiritual strength

A more positive outlook on life

A better sense of humor

Growth in charity

Growth in compassion

Better relationships with others

Becoming more God-like

the essence of prayer is intention, not attentio.

Be Like Water

Water is fluid, flexible. It flows around obstacles, under or over obstacles. It flows down to the lowest level (humility is willing to be at the lowest level - like Jesus). The water in a river or lake is available for drinking, cooking, or washing to anyone (universal charity).

Be flexible, humble, loving through regular prayer.

essence of prayer is intention, not attention

d. Simply Praying

Praying is simple and easy. Many books make prayer complicated or seem difficult. If you can talk, you can pray. If you can think, you can pray. This little book will explain the essence of prayer and how to pray simply. It will guide you to the highest form of prayer, which is the simplest form of prayer. Use this book as a manual, a workbook, to guide you step by step, day by day. Praying well takes consistent practice. Praying simply takes consistent practice.

Praying simply will encourage you to pray more often, and will increase your inner peace. Love is the essence, the nature, of God, but His primary trait is simplicity. This trait of simplicity is the reason there is only ONE God, and not three Gods. Praying simply will help you to become simpler in your spiritual life, and thus you will resemble God more closely

In your relationship with God, nothing is more important than your prayer life. The deeper your prayer life is, the more intimate your relationship with God will be. Prayer opens your mind, heart, and soul to receive God's love, wisdom, and strength, day by day. In all your relationships, your prayer life serves as a foundation of peace, patience, and forgiveness.

the essence of prayer is intention, not attentio

Most of the Christian guidelines and suggestions in this book are based on "The Cloud of Unknowing" and "Book of Privy Counsel" by an unknown English Carthusian monk of the 14th century, and drawn from the writings of St. John of the Cross and St. Teresa of Avila. Become God's Blessing to everyone: family members, friends, acquaintances, fellow workers, everyone you meet. Through a deeper prayer life, you can be a source of God's acceptance, affirmation, comfort, compassion, forgiveness, love, and peace to everyone. As God's Blessing, you empower, energize, enrich the heart and spirit of others. The Blessings you receive from God and from others enable you to be a Blessing to others. Be aware of these Blessings to help you be a Blessing to others.

e essence of prayer is intention, not attention

e. The Practice of Prayer

- Praying is a privilege.
- Every prayer is a gift from God, an invitation to receive God's love and blessings.
- Short frequent payers make our whole life prayerful.
- For God, nothing about us is trivial. Our trivial prayers are important to Him, and are signs of our humility and reliance on Him.
- Often we do not understand the full impact of what we are praying.
- The Holy Spirit is in control of our praying: He starts it, sustains it, and answers it.
- Short frequent intense prayers lead to longer periods of prayer.
- Be available for prayer at any time.
- St. Anthony the Great: "The best prayer of all is when we are unaware that we are praying during prayer."
- Pray with freedom in simplicity and gentleness.
- Frequent prayers of petition lead to a greater awareness of God's presence.

the essence of prayer is intention, not attentio

• Pray the prayer in your heart with humility and trust, and let God deal with it.

"Giving thanks always for all things in the name of Our Lord Jesus Christ to God the Father." Eph. 5:20

• Gratitude enlarges the heart for loving and for receiving blessings.

• The foundation for longer periods of prayer is frequent intense prayers.

• Liturgical prayer (with many of the Psalms) is the official prayer of the Whole Christ, Christ the Head and His Mystical Body.

• Jesus referred to Psalms at key parts of His life.

• The Liturgy (the Mass, Sacraments, liturgy of hours) enlarges our heart and conforms it to the Heart of Christ.

• The Liturgy reflects the many moods of Jesus, and the many moods of our relationship with God.

• In the Sacrifice of the Mass we give ourselves totally to God, and then we are consecrated and transformed into Christ spiritually.

e essence of prayer is intention, not attention

f. The Spirit of Prayer

The Holy Spirit is the Spirit of Prayer.

Why?

1) Because He is the Spirit of Love.
   True prayer comes from the heart –
   heart speaks to heart.

2) Prayer is union with God; praying is
   bonding with God.

   The Holy Spirit is the Bond of Love

   between the Father and the Son,

   between God and each person.

   During prayer the Holy Spirit
   is bonding us to God

3) He is the Spirit of Silence – silence is the
   language of God, and the language of love.

4) *The Holy Spirit gave Jesus the spirit of
   prayer to enable Him to pray
   "Without Ceasing" (1Thess.5:17).*

   We need the spirit of prayer from the Spirit
   of Prayer to deepen our prayer life, to pray
   "Without Ceasing".

the essence of prayer is intention, not attentio

"But in like manner the Spirit also helps our weakness. For do not know what we should pray for as we ought, but the Spirit himself pleads for us with unutterable groanings. And he who searches hearts knows what the Spirit desires, that he pleads for the saints according to God." Rom. 8:26-27

"Holy Spirit, teach us how to pray, help us in our prayer life".

essence of prayer is intention, not attention

g. Kinds of Prayer

The essence of prayer is union with God.
St. Thomas wrote that "the minimum requirement
for prayer is intention, not attention."

A Form or Manner:
- Communal
  Liturgical: The Mass, Sacraments, Divine Office
  Devotional: The Rosary, Novenas, etc.

- Personal
  Vocal: With a formula or spontaneous
  Mental: Meditation, spontaneous,
  prayer of simplicity

- Contemplative:
  Active contemplation
  Passive contemplation

B Intention (motive)

C Person addressed: The Father, Jesus,
  Holy Spirit, Blessed Mother, Saints, or angels.

The benefits
of prayer happen
independently

of how it went,
what you think,
or how you feel

h. Liturgical Prayer

Liturgical Prayer is the official prayer of the entire Mystical Body of Christ, Head and members. The Risen Christ is the Head of this Mystical Body, and all Christians form His Body.

"For as the body is one and has many members, and all the members of the body, many as they are, form one body, so also it is with Christ." 1 Cor 12: 12

"Now you are the body of Christ, member for member." 1 Cor 12:27

"Again, he is the head of his body, the Church;" Col 1:18

the essence of prayer is intention, not attentio

All the prayers offered to the Father by Jesus while on earth are stored in His Mind and Heart. Liturgical Prayer is the praying of the Risen Christ in and through His Mystical Body. Whenever we offer the Sacrifice of the Mass, or take part in the Sacraments, or pray the Liturgy of Hours, we join in the praying of the Risen Christ. Continually throughout the world, the Mass is being offered, the Sacraments are being administered, and the Divine Office is being prayed by monks, nuns, priests, and lay people. The Risen Christ inheaven is continually interceding for us all.

This is the reason Liturgical Prayer is so powerful and so important.

Join in the Liturgical Prayer of the Whole Christ.

You join in this Liturgical Prayer of the Whole Christ and His redeeming activity whenever you take part in the Mass or Sacraments or the Divine Office.

e essence of prayer is intention, not attention

The Mystical Body of Christ (Christ the Head and the Church) is the extension of the Person of Christ through time and space.

The Liturgy (the Mass, Sacraments, and Divine Office) is the extension of the Redeeming Activity of Christ through time and space.

The Liturgy is like the earth's magnetic field which:

- holds in and preserves our atmosphere so essential for all life and climate;
- protects earth from lethal solar flares and cosmic rays;
- keeps in the ozone layer that protects all life from lethal UV light;
- enables the migration of birds and animals, and navigation;
- protects our satellites and electric/electronic grids;
- yet lets in sunlight for life.

The daily Mass, Sacraments, and Divine Office give and preserve the spiritual life of people on earth, provide spiritual nourishment, and protect them from spiritual dangers.

the essence of prayer is intention, not attentio

Ⓑ Understanding Prayer

a. Questions

b. Answers

c. Basic Realities

d. Notes on Prayer

e. Having the Right Intention

f. The Healing Power of God Within Me

g. God's Healing and Help

h. Being Open to God

e essence of prayer is intention, not attention

Quiz / True or False

a. Questions

1 ◯ Distractions during prayer are natural and normal.

2 ◯ Our daily living should be brought into our praying.

3 ◯ Praying is easy to do.

4 ◯ Inner restlessness indicates a need for prayer.

5 ◯ The way we live affects the way we pray.

the essence of prayer is intention, not attentio

b. Answers

1. Distractions during prayer are natural and normal.
   True. Distractions during prayer are natural and normal. We do not have complete control over our mind, and God knows that.

2. Our daily living should be brought into our praying.
   True. The needs and incidents of daily living provide the contents of our prayers.

3. Praying is easy to do.
   True. Praying is just as easy as playing golf or playing tennis (badly). But praying well is difficult, just as playing golf or tennis well is difficult.

4. Inner restlessness indicates a need for prayer.
   True. Inner restless results from a guilty conscience or stress or worry. In these situations, prayer is needed to seek forgiveness, inner peace, or God's help.

5. The way we live affects the way we pray.
   True. A sinful life makes praying difficult. A hectic, chaotic life makes praying difficult. A materialistic (greedy) life makes praying difficult.

e essence of prayer is intention, not attention

a. Questions

6　◯　Prayer is mainly a spiritual union of minds with God

7　◯　The goal of prayer is to possess God.

8　◯　Praying is both simple and complex.

the essence of prayer is intention, not attentio

b. Answers

6. Prayer is mainly a spiritual union of minds with God.
   False, because prayer is mainly a spiritual union of wills with God, and secondarily a union of minds with God. This is the reason that distractions do not end our praying, because our wills are still united to God's will. We stop praying only when we deliberately decide to stop praying. God knows we do not have complete control over our mind. Do not expect more than what God expects.

7. The goal of prayer is to possess God.
   False. How can a drop of water possess (contain) the ocean? The goal of prayer is to be possessed by God.

8. Praying is both simple and complex.
   True. Praying can be simple with complicated factors involved, such as the degree of faith, humility, and love, the motive, preparation, etc.

e essence of prayer is intention, not attention

21

a. Questions

9 ○ Progress in prayer means becoming more active in prayer.

10 ○ Giving reasons is important in prayer.

11 ○ God answers every prayer in a positive way (a "no" is negative).

the essence of prayer is intention, not attentio

b. Answers

9. Progress in prayer means becoming more active in prayer.

   False. Progress in praying means to become more simple and more passive. The highest form of prayer is achieved when a person is passively allowing the Holy Spirit to pray in and through her or him.

10. Giving reasons is important in prayer.

    True. When asking God for others or for self, we should reason with God. Tell Him the reasons for the need or the request.

11. God answers every prayer in a positive way (a "no" is negative).

    True, because God answers every prayer in one of three ways:

    1) by giving us what we ask for; or

    2) by giving it to us later; or

    3) by giving us something else instead when He says no to what we ask for.

essence of prayer is intention, not attention

a. Questions

12 ◯ God talks back to us during prayer.

13 ◯ Sin is the greatest obstacle to prayer.

the essence of prayer is intention, not attentio

b. Answers

12. God talks back to us during prayer.
    True. God responds by influencing our mind, emotions, memory, imagination, or will.

13. Sin is the greatest obstacle to prayer.
    False. We are all sinners. The only obstacle to prayer is the refusal to pray because of pride, indifference, or being too busy.

e essence of prayer is intention, not attention

c. Basic Realities

That should influence, guide and transform my prayer life.

God is the beginning, middle, and end of my prayer-life.

He starts, sustains and completes it.

"I am quite certain that the One who began this good work in you will bring it to completion when the Day of Christ arrives." Phil. 1:6

the essence of prayer is intention, not attentio

- In prayer, we are NOT the seeker, the pursuer, the hunter; but the one sought, pursued, and hunted by God.

"Look, I am standing at the door, knocking. If anyone hears me calling and opens the door, I will come in to share his meal, side by side with him." Rev. 3:20

- In prayer, listen to what God is saying to you, and then respond.

"The Spirit too comes to help us in our weakness. For when we cannot choose words in order to pray properly, the Spirit Himself expresses our pleas in a way that could never be put into words, and God who knows everything in our hearts knows perfectly well what he means, and that the pleas of the saints expressed by the Spirit are according to the mind of God." Rom. 8:26-27

- In prayer, be free and willing to be led by the Holy Spirit.

e essence of prayer is intention, not attention

Fidelity and flexibility should be traits of my prayer life.

  A. Fidelity is lived out by praying regularly.

  B. Flexibility is achieved

    1. In oneself through

      a. freedom from anxiety and anxiousness about prayer

      b. being relaxed immediately before prayer and during prayer.

    2. In method through readiness to use any one of a variety of prayer forms.

  C. Immediacy should be the primary trait of my union with God in prayer.

  Immediacy in space = oneness

"Make your home in me, as I make mine in you. As a branch cannot bear fruit all by itself, but must remain part of the vine, neither can you unless you remain in me. I am the vine; you are the branches. Whoever remains in me, with me in him, bears fruit in plenty, for cut off from me you can do nothing." John 15:4-5

"It is now no longer I who live, but Christ lives in me." Gal. 2:20

the essence of prayer is intention, not attentio

D. Immediacy in time = NOW, the present moment.

The past doesn't matter, the future doesn't exist.

The only thing that is real and that matters is the present moment.

God's presence right now is more real and more important than His presence in the past or in the future.

We can experience God directly (immediately) only right NOW.

"If you are depressed, you are living in the past.
If you are anxious, you are living in the future.
If you are at peace, you are living in the present."
Lao Tzu

E. Immediacy in manner (in spirit) = a simple, direct experience of God without the mediation of:

   1. words

   2. images

   3. concepts

   4. emotions

   5. thoughts

essence of prayer is intention, not attention

I breathe in God's peace,
which heals and soothes me.
I breathe in God's strength,
which empowers me.
I breathe in God's light,
which brightens my life.
I breathe in God's love,
which fills my whole being.

the essence of prayer is intention, not attentio

d. Notes on Prayer

If you're one of those who feel as though you don't pray well, I think the following, based on the writing of Abbot John Chapman (1862-1932), might be of some help.

1. "Pray as you can, and don't try to pray as you cannot. Take yourself as you find yourself."

2. "The only way to pray is to pray; and the way to pray well is to pray much. The less one prays the worse it goes."

3. "If you have no time to pray much, at least pray regularly."

4. "If you must put up with the fact that when you do try to pray, you can't seem to get into it, then let your prayer consist of telling this to God."

5. "Begin wherever you find yourself. Make any acts you want to make and feel you ought to make, but do not force yourself into, feelings of any kind."

e essence of prayer is intention, not attention

6. "If you don't know what to do when you have a quarter of an hour alone in Church, then shut out everything else and just give yourself to God and beg Him to have mercy on you and offer Him all your distractions."

7. "You can't get rid of the worries of this world or of the questionings of the intellect, but you can laugh at them. Laugh at yourself and then think of God. In the simple relation you have with God by prayer, it is as though you are in the center of a wheel where the noise of the revolving circumference does not matter."

8. "In the simple relation you have with God by prayer, it is as though you are in the center of a wheel where the noise of the revolving circumference does not matter."

the essence of prayer is intention, not attentio

e. Having the Right Intention

1. Pray in order to give yourself to God.

2. Pure prayer is a prayer of the will; it is pure intention without words. Do not worry about what you should think or feel. Think about your intention to give yourself to God, cling to Him. Feelings are useful for beginners, but they are not to be depended on. Do not mind commotion or rebellion. Just pray that you may cling to God in absolute detachment.

3. Reason is necessary for theology and ordinary conduct but in prayer it is only useful for beginners. You do not have to reason that God is to be loved, except in the early stages.

4. Want what He wants. Inner quiet is necessary for peace. But if God does not wish us to have peace we must be satisfied with confusion. So do not worry about reasoning your way into God's presence, which is peace of an elusive kind.

e essence of prayer is intention, not attention

5. If we prayed simply because we wanted the "consolations of religion," the state of things would be very disappointing. But if we pray in order to give ourselves to God just as we are, then our imperfections at prayer at any given moment are what God wants. Granted it is not the very best we can do, but in general it is the only kind of prayer we can pray. Even if it is far from what we want, it is what God wants.

6. For those who love God all things work together toward the good. Every circumstance in life is a means to getting to heaven, and a part of God's Providence. So that at every moment we are in touch with God, including the times when we have feelings of distraction and are unable to pray peacefully.

7. Minimize what happens in your own soul and maximize God's love for you. Do not think that distraction, dryness and desolation are merely stages of a trial which you pass through on your way to perfection. Perfection in this world is not a calm union with God, unless God so wishes. Jesus suffered temptation and desolation to show us that they are not incompatible with perfection, but in fact are part of perfection. Progress will be made when we become more and more indifferent as to what state we are in.

the essence of prayer is intention, not attentio

8. Do not try to be simple, God does that for you.
Your part is:
  • to think of others;
  • to be with God;
  • to avoid thinking about your own "spiritual state."

9. Simply be what God enables you to be at this moment. God is not only in every external event, but in every internal event, in every involuntary feeling you have — at every moment in your life you are in touch with God, and His hand is on you. You have only to be carried in His arms. Your one care must be not to jump free and try to walk alone; and finally when you are certain of His love, enjoy the Lord.

10. You need not expect to be successful in these efforts. You need only to repeat that you want God's will. And if you must bear some form of suffering, physical, emotional or mental, do not get down on yourself. It is not against perfection to feel that suffering is intolerable, and it is all right to tell God that it is intolerable. Only try with the highest part of you to trust Him and be willing to suffer as long as He chooses, knowing that He will give you the necessary grace.

essence of prayer is intention, not attention

f. The Healing Power of God Within Me

"Do you not know that you are the temple of God, and that the Spirit of God dwells in you?" I Cor 3:16

Because God is within me
at the center of my soul,
I will allow Him to heal me from within.

"For I, the Lord, am your healer." Ex. 15:26

Because God is within me,
at the center of my soul,
I will seek Him within myself through prayer.

Because God is found in the midst of peace,
I will calm my inner self
with slow deep breathing
before praying.

Because God within awaits and welcomes me,
I will seek Him within myself through prayer,
often, anywhere, and anytime.

Because God within loves everyone,
I will let His love flow out
from me to everyone.

the essence of prayer is intention, not attentio

g. God's Healing and Help

*"Let nothing disturb you; nothing cause you fear;
all things pass. God is unchanging. Patience obtains
all; whoever has God needs nothing else. God alone
suffices." (Bookmark of St. Teresa of Avila)*

Through prayer, my union with God within me will:

- heal the wounds of my past pains
- purify me of arrogance and selfishness
- increase my inner strength and courage
- teach me patience and endurance
- deepen my faith and trust in God
- give me peace of mind, peace of heart,
  and peace of soul
- expand my love for God and for others.

*"How great is your goodness, O Lord,
which you have in store for those who fear you."
Psalm 31:20*

e essence of prayer is intention, not attention

h. Being Open to God

Because prayer opens my mind, heart, and soul to God, I will receive God's Goodness through prayer. I can use any one of these, or make up my own.

God's Peace

As I inhale slowly and deeply, mentally I say,
I breathe in God's peace;

As I exhale slowly, mentally I say,
I breathe out tension.

As I inhale slowly and deeply, mentally I say,
I breathe in God's peace;

As I exhale slowly, mentally I say,
I breathe out worry.

As I inhale slowly and deeply, mentally I say,
1 breathe in God's peace;

As I exhale slowly, mentally I say,
I breathe out anxiety.

As I inhale slowly and deeply, mentally I say,
I breathe in God's peace;

As I exhale slowly, mentally I say,
I breathe out my fears.

the essence of prayer is intention, not attentio

As I inhale slowly and deeply, mentally I say,
I breathe in God's peace;

As I exhale slowly, mentally I say,
I breathe out irritation.

As I inhale slowly and deeply, mentally I say,
I breathe in God's peace,

As I exhale slowly, mentally I say,
I breathe out turmoil.

e essence of prayer is intention, not attention

ⓒ My Inner Journey to God

"For we are the temple of the living God;
As God said, "I will live in them and move among
them, and I will be their God,
and they shall be my people." 2 Cor 6:16

a. My Need for Prayer

b. My Need for God

c. The Breath of Life

d. The Healer Within

e. Relaxing My Body for Prayer

f. Calming My Inner Self for Prayer

g. The Need for Inner Peace

h. My Daily Contact with God

the essence of prayer is intention, not attentio

a. My Need for Prayer

"Take heed, watch and pray." Mark 13:33

    Why am I so restless?

    Why do I feel so troubled or anxious?

    How can I find and experience God within me?

    What is blocking my path to God within me?

    Is it my work ?

    Other people ?

    Myself?

e essence of prayer is intention, not attention

b. My Need for God

"The Lord is my light and my salvation;
whom should I fear?
The Lord is my life's refuge;
of whom should I be afraid?" Psalm 27:1

Sometimes I feel empty inside.
I feel this longing for something unknown.
After a while, I tire of things.
After a while, I tire of people.

"Because You have made us for Thyself, O Lord, our hearts are restless until they rest in Thee." St. Augustine

the essence of prayer is intention, not attentio

c. The Breath of Life

"The Lord God formed man out of dust from the ground, and breathed into his nostrils the breath of life." Gen 2:7

I will use slow deep breathing to gain control of my mind and body, as a preparation for prayer.

My slow deep breathing will join brain, body, heart, ands spirit for a closer union with God.

My slow deep breathing will strengthen the force and flow of the spiritual energy that comes from God.

Breathe on us, Breath of God,
until our hearts are pure,
until with You we have one will,
to live and to endure.

Breath on us, Breath of God,
our souls with grace refine,
until this earthly part of us
glows with fire divine.

Breathe on us, Breath of God,
fill us with life anew,
that we may love the things You love,
and do what You would do.

Breathe on us, Breath of God,
so we shall never die,
but give You thanks and praise
throughout eternity. Amen

e essence of prayer is intention, not attention

d. The Healer Within

"For I, the Lord, am your healer." Ex 15:26

Because God is within me
at the center of my soul,
I will allow Him to heal me from within.

I will use a low deep breathing
to calm my inner self,
so God can heal me.

I will calm my mind, emotions, and heart,
so God can heal my mind, emotions, and heart
from the wounds of sin and selfishness.

I will use relaxation techniques,
so God's presence within me will be free
to energize me.

the essence of prayer is intention, not attentio

e. Relaxing My Body for Prayer

"Do you not know that your body is a temple of the Holy Spirit within you, whom you have from God, and that you are not your own?" I Cor 6:19

"Therefore, glorify God in your body." I Cor 6:20

Raise your arms straight up with palms facing frontward, and then stretch upward on tiptoes as high as you can. Do this three times.

With your arms hanging as limp as wet towels, swing your arms left and right by twisting your hips and torso left and right. Do seven to ten sets of this.

Gently and slowly lower your head forward as far down as it will go, as if to touch your collarbone with your chin. Hold for five seconds.

Gently and slowly pull your head backward as far back as it will go. Hold for five seconds. Repeat this forward and backward stretching of your neck muscles three times.

e essence of prayer is intention, not attention

With shoulders relaxed and arms hanging
limp, rotate your head slowly in wide
smooth circles seven to ten times.
Then do the same thing in the opposite
direction.

With shoulders relaxed and arms hanging limp,
slowly rotate your shoulders forward
in wide smooth circles seven to ten times.
Do the same thing with a backward rotation.

the essence of prayer is intention, not attentio

f. Calming My Inner Self for Prayer

*"Quiet! Be still! The wind ceased
and there was a great calm." Mark 4:39*

After relaxing your body, sit comfortably
with a straight back to balance your head,
and then do deep breathing (abdominal breathing)
in this manner:

I will inhale slowly from the bottom
of my lungs upward
for a relaxed breath,
pause briefly,
and then exhale slowly.

While inhaling slowly, I mentally count one;
while exhaling slowly, I mentally count one.
When I reach ten, I will begin another set
of ten relaxed breaths.

Doing three, five, or more of these sets
of ten breaths will:

- dissolve tension,

- lower my blood pressure,

- allow inner healing,

- refresh my body, mind, heart, and spirit,

- prepare me for prayer.

essence of prayer is intention, not attention

g. The Need for Inner Peace

Inner peace is essential for a deeper prayer life and the practice of Charity.

"Charity is patient, is kind; does not envy, is not pretentious, is not puffed up, is not ambitious, is not self-seeking, is not provoked; thinks no evil, does not rejoice over wickedness, but rejoices with the truth; bears with all things, believes all things, hopes all things, endures all all things." 1 Cor 13:4-7

the essence of prayer is intention, not attentio

The Three Levels of Inner Peace

Peace of mind
calmness in the mind

Peace of heart
calmness in the emotions

Peace of soul
calmness in the soul from a
clear conscience with God and with others

(Peace of soul is the most important because it
helps us to "survive" despite turmoil in the mind
and turmoil in the emotions.)

e essence of prayer is intention, not attention

h. My Daily Contact with God

"Peace I leave with you; my peace I give to you."
John 14:27

Whenever the need arises —
at home, at work, or elsewhere —
I will use the following prayer:

As I inhale slowly and deeply, mentally I say,
"I breathe in God's peace;"

As I exhale slowly, mentally I say,
"I breathe out tension."

Or

As I inhale slowly and deeply, mentally I say,
"I breathe in God's peace;"

As I exhale slowly, mentally I say,
"I breathe out worry."

After doing this for three or five minutes,
I will be calm, clear, and centered
with God's peace.

As I calm my inner self and breathe in God's peace,
God will envelop me
with the embrace of His peace.

the essence of prayer is intention, not attentio

D The Commotion Within

"Though distress and anguish have come upon me, your commands are my delight." Psalm 119: 143

   a. Why all the Commotion?
   b. Praying with the Commotion
   c. Can Emotions Block My Prayer?
   d. Dealing with My Emotions
   e. Directing the Inner Flow for Prayer

e essence of prayer is intention, not attention

a. Why All the Commotion?

"Amen, amen, I say to you, you will weep and mourn, while the world rejoices; you will grieve, but your grief will become joy." John 16:20

As inner reactions to a person, event, or situation, my emotions are gauges that inform or warn me about what is happening.

My emotions also provide me with opportunities for building internal strength and for prayer.

My emotions have a life of their own, an intelligence of their own.

The emotional flow of my life is like:
the engine in my car
the wind in my sail
the colors in my favorite painting
the rhythm in my favorite music
the love I have for others

.

I will respect and accept the flow of my emotions.

the essence of prayer is intention, not attentio

b. Praying with the Commotion

*"Rejoice in hope, endure in affliction,
persevere in prayer." Rom 12:12*

Because my emotions are non-rational, non-logical,
there's no need to understand
or describe them clearly.

Because I have no direct control over my emotions,
I will deal with them indirectly

Because my emotional states are temporary,
I will allow time for them to quiet down,
cool down.

Because all my emotions are God-given and good,
I will accept all my emotions, even negative ones.

I will remind myself that there is no need
for guilt feelings
for having negative emotions,
because all my emotions are good.

I will pray with my emotions,
from my emotions,
and because of my emotions.

Because the best prayers come from the heart,
I will speak to God from my heart.

essence of prayer is intention, not attention

c. Can Emotions Block My Prayer?

"Neither death, nor life, nor angels, nor principalities, nor present things, nor future things, nor powers, nor height, nor depth, nor any other creature will be able to separate us from the love of God in Christ Jesus our Lord." Rom 8:38-39

None of my emotions can stop me from praying.

Like physical pain, my negative emotions are unpleasant and undesirable, but absolutely necessary for my survival, growth, and development.

Fear triggers my flight or fight response, which helps me to survive physically, psychologically, and spiritually.

Fear of consequences motivates me to get something done, and enables me to do it quickly to meet a deadline.

Hurt feelings and disappointments can help me to strengthen my relationships.

Feelings of depression can help me to develop internal and spiritual strength

I will respect and accept all my negative emotions as helpful gauges for surviving, growing, improving my skills, and helping my prayer life.

the essence of prayer is intention, not attentic

d. Dealing with My Emotions

"Let all bitterness and wrath and anger and clamor and slander be put away from you, with all malice." Eph 4:31

I will use healthy outlets for my strong emotions:

- exercise or sports
- craft or hobby
- the arts
- talking it out with a friend
- positive humor

Because I have no direct control over my emotions, I will deal with them indirectly.

Dealing with my emotions directly makes them stronger or last longer.

The best way of removing the air from a container is to fill the container with water.

I will remove my negative feelings by replacing them with other feelings by doing something that holds my total attention, or by praying.

I will change the way I feel by changing what I'm thinking, saying, or doing, or by praying.

e essence of prayer is intention, not attention

e. Directing the Inner Flow for Prayer

"Persevere in prayer, being watchful in it with thanksgiving." Col 4:2

I can direct the flow of my emotions by:

- focusing my attention on this or that,
- talking about this or that,
- doing this or that.

I will gain greater control over my emotions by directing the use of my:

- external senses —
  sight, hearing, smell, touch, taste;

- inner faculties —
  simple reasoning, memory, imagination, emotions;

- spiritual powers — intellect and free will.

I will learn to direct the flow of my emotions to preserve my peace within and to pray better.

I will use the relaxation technique of slow deep breathing to calm the commotion within for praying better.

the essence of prayer is intention, not attentio

E Obstacles to Prayer

"I am the way, and the truth, and the life."
John 14:6

a. The God of Reality

b. Self-made Obstacles

c. A Forgiving God

d. Praying with Distractions

e. God Here and Now

Benefits of Prayer

The Spirit of Prayer

essence of prayer is intention, not attention

a. The God of Reality

"God said to Moses, I AM WHO I AM" Ex. 3:14

The past events of my life no longer exist.
They're gone.

The future does not actually exist.
It may exist in my mind or imagination
only as thoughts or imaginings.

I was regretting the past and
fearing the future.

Suddenly God was speaking:
"My Name is I AM."

I waited. God continued:
"When you live in the past,
with its mistakes and regrets,
it is hard; I am not there.
My Name is not I Was".

"When you live in the future,
with its problems and fears, it is hard;
I am not there. My Name is not I Will Be".

"When you live in this moment,
it is not hard; I am here.
My Name is " I AM. "

Helen Mallicoat

Because God is present within me this moment,
I pray to God here and now.

the essence of prayer is intention, not attentio

b. Self-made Obstacles

"My grace is sufficient for you, for my power is made perfect in weakness." 2 Cor 12:9

Focusing on:

- my mistakes
- my weaknesses
- mistreatment from others
- injustices suffered

· will lead me to self-pity.

Seeking pity by telling others about my struggles and misfortunes leads me to self-pity.

Because God cannot be found in the mud of self-pity, I will focus on God present within me.

Because of God's immense love for me, I will pray to God present within me.

c. A Forgiving God

"For you, O Lord, are good and forgiving, abounding in kindness to all who call upon you." Psalm 86:5

After seeking forgiveness from God for my sins,
I will let go of my guilt feelings.

If God forgives me,
why should I refuse to forgive myself?
That is, refuse to let go of my guilt feelings?

I will not allow feelings of guilt
to deter me from praying,
because I refuse to focus on my sins.

When feelings of guilt return,
I will thank God for His forgiveness,
and talk to Him about other things.

Because God is so loving and merciful,
I will never allow my sins or guilt to
prevent me from praying.

d. Praying with Distractions

"Rejoice always. Pray without ceasing.
In all circumstances give thanks." 1 Thes 5:16-18

Distractions during prayer
frustrate and discourage many people.

Because prayer is mainly a union of my will
with God's will, I am still praying
if my distractions are not deliberate.

Because God knows I do not have complete control
over my mind and thoughts,
He accepts my distractions
as part of my prayer.

Because distractions are part of my praying,
I will never allow distractions
to discourage me from praying.

I will do slow deep breathing to calm my inner
self as a preparation for praying.

e essence of prayer is intention, not attention

While praying, if I do my best, God will do the rest

the essence of prayer is intention, not attentio

Praying is about intention not attention

essence of prayer is intention, not attention

e. God Here and Now

"Behold, now is the acceptable time;
behold, now is the day of salvation." 2 Cor 6:2

Because past events and future events
do not exist in reality,
I will find the God of reality
only in the present.

Living in the present moment
keeps me in touch with God
here and now.

God invented the flow of time
to prevent everything
from happening all at once.

Because the present moment is small and
manageable, praying here and now is easy and
manageable.

Because God is "I AM",
in the present moment,
I pray to God here and now.

the essence of prayer is intention, not attentio

Benefits of Prayer

St. Paul: "Prayer leads to what is true, honorable, just, pure, lovely, gracious, excellent, praiseworthy."

St. Catherine of Siena: "By humble and faithful prayer, the soul acquires, with time and perseverance, every virtue."

St. Bernard: "Prayer preserves peace of soul because it":

- "regulates our emotions"
- "directs our actions"
- "corrects our faults"
- "guides our behavior"
- "puts order in our life"
- "beautifies our life"
- "gives knowledge about people and relationships"
- "gives knowledge about God and our relationship with God"

essence of prayer is intention, not attention

The Spirit of Prayer

The Holy Spirit is the Spirit of Prayer.

Why? Because He is the Spirit of Love.
True prayer comes from the heart –
heart speaks to heart.

He is the Spirit of Silence – silence is
the language of God, and the language of love.

Prayer is union with God;
praying is bonding with God.

The Holy Spirit is the Bond of Love
between the Father and the Son,
between God and each person.

During prayer the Holy Spirit
is bonding us to God.

*The Holy Spirit gave Jesus the spirit of prayer to
enable Him to pray "without ceasing". 1 Thess. 5:17*

We need the spirit of prayer
from the Spirit of Prayer
to deepen our prayer life,
to pray "without ceasing".

the essence of prayer is intention, not attentio

"But in like manner the Spirit also helps our weakness. For do not know what we should pray for as we ought, but the Spirit himself pleads for us with unutterable groanings. And he who searches hearts knows what the Spirit desires, that he pleads for the saints according to God". Rom. 8:26-27

"Holy Spirit,

teach us how to pray,

help us in our prayer life."

e essence of prayer is intention, not attention

Consecration to the Holy Spirit
Serenity Prayers

Prayer purifies

the essence of prayer is intention, not attention

1. Beginners must read spiritual books, reflect, and pray often.

2. True sorrow for sin is important for prayer and contemplation.

3. Being free of sin and having patience are needed for deeper prayer.

4. Forcing, straining, is not helpful in the spiritual life.

5. Practice prayer and contemplation with a quiet, gentle spirit.

6. Each person has her/his own path and own experience of prayer and contemplation.

7. Prayer and contemplation are openness to God and His Blessings.

8. God awakens and touches the soul in different ways.

9. God is not His works. God is God.

10. "Taste and see the goodness of God" ≑ Experience and know the goodness of God.

e essence of prayer is intention, not attention

11. The work of grace =
    the activity of the Holy Spirit.

12. St.Teresa of Avila: "There are four ways to water a garden (of prayer)":

    a "By hand with water from a well."

    b "Use a water wheel to draw water into a trough that carries the water to the garden."

    c "By irrigation from a running stream near the garden."

    d "Let it rain."

13. St. Thomas Aquinas: "There are two kinds of knowledge, so there are two kinds of prayer":

    a "Acquired knowledge with scientific inquiry using senses, faculties, and intellect — active contemplation."

    b "A Gift of Wisdom from the Holy Spirit —ˆ infused contemplation."

Prayer enlightens

the essence of prayer is intention, not attentio

14. St. Gregory of Palamas, the St. Thomas Aquinas of the Eastern Church (in his book "Theology of Light") states three kinds of light:

   a "Sensible — physical"

   b "Intellectual - mental"

   c "Uncreated — divine energy that can overflow onto the senses, faculties, and powers. At Mt. Tabor Jesus radiated uncreated energy as light."

15. Heb. 12:29 "Our God is the consuming fire." This inner fire is the uncreated energy of God. Why not allow this inner fire of God to encompass your entire being?

Prayer is creative

essence of prayer is intention, not attention

16. Evagrius the Solitary (345 - 399 AD):
"A theologian is one who prays,
and the one who prays is a theologian.

17. St. Teresa of Avila: "There are three
separate abilities:"

   a "Receive a grace"

   b "Understand it"

   c "Express it with words"

18. Bernard Lonergan (1904-84) —Transcendental
Precepts from "Method in Theology":

   a "Be Attentive"

   b "Be Intelligent"

   c "Be Reasonable"

   d "Be-in-Love"

   e "Be Lovingly Attentive, Lovingly Intelligent,
   Lovingly Responsible

Prayer transcends

the essence of prayer is intention, not attentio

19. Our social crisis of faith comes from a weak Culture of Faith. To best understand Catholic spirituality, experience good Catholic Art and read the lives of the Saints.

20. The "Purgative Way" is the path of purification from sin and sinful inclinations. It is a path of liberation, which lasts till death. This purification and liberation come from Christ's Passion and Resurrection.

Prayer liberates

e essence of prayer is intention, not attention

21. When sexuality and the sex drive are transcended and transformed by grace, its energy longs for union with God. All mystics are creative.

22. The 7 Gifts of the Holy Spirit are given for service and help for others.

    What have I done for God (Christ)?

    What am I doing for God (Christ)?

    What should do I do for God (Christ)?

23. There is a social dimension to prayer and contemplation. Micah 6:8 "And what does the Lord require of you but to do justice, and to love kindness, and to walk humbly with your God."

Prayer is a gift you give to yourself

the essence of prayer is intention, not attentio

Consecration to the Holy Spirit

O Holy Spirit, Divine Spirit of light and love, I consecrate to You my understanding, heart, and will for time and for eternity. May my understanding be always submissive to Your inspiration. Inflame my heart with love for God and for others. Conform my will to the Divine Will, and help me to live out the life and virtues of Jesus – His purity, humility, and charity – to Whom with the Father and You be honor and glory forever. Amen.

essence of prayer is intention, not attention

Serenity Prayers

Lord, grant me the serenity to accept the things I cannot change, courage to change the things I can, and wisdom to know the difference.

the essence of prayer is intention, not attentio

Lord, grant me the serenity to accept the people I cannot stand; courage to change the ones I can; and wisdom to know I am the only one I can change.

essence of prayer is intention, not attention

Part 2
CHALLENGES

As you read,
as you learn
to pray, as you
go through life,
above you the
Holy Spirit will
always be there
to help

Holy Spirit

You

The essence of prayer is intention, not attention

the essence of prayer is intention, not attentio

It's important that you pray often and regularly, but it doesn't matter how you pray.

Prayer is union with God, being with God.

Praying is like being in a small sailboat with God steering and the Holy Spirit blowing it along.

The following factors do not change the reality of your being with God, your praying:

- smooth, choppy, or stormy sea;
  (your state of mind and/or emotional state)

- calm, changing, or blustery winds;
  (your situation and/or circumstances of life)

- various sea birds or creatures coming or going;
  (the distractions that come and go)

- whether you're alert or not, comfortable or not, fearful or not; (your physical-psychological state)

- whether you're talking to God or just being silent.

You are praying because you are with God.
God accepts you as you are, no matter your situation or your circumstances.

essence of prayer is intention, not attention

While praying:

- Whether your state of mind or emotional state is smooth, choppy, or stormy does not matter.
- Whether your present situation or circumstances of life is calm, changing, or blustery does not matter.
- Whether few or many distractions come or go does not matter.
- Whether you're alert or drowsy, with comfort, discomfort or pain, fearful or calm does not matter.

the essence of prayer is intention, not attentio

A Praying for Others

"May the Lord make you increase and abound in love for one another and for all, just as we have for you."
1 Thes 3:12

    a. Toxic Grudges

    b. Difficult Grudges

    c. The Way of Forgiveness

    d. Praying for My Foes

    e. The Peace of Acceptance

    f. Bonding Through Prayer

    g. Prayers of Love

    Abbot John Chapman – with comments

    The Spirit of Freedom

    The Jesus Prayer

    Two Zen Monks

    Father Damien of Molokai

    Lectio Divina

    The Sacred Liturgy ad the Mystery of our Redemption

    Prayer of Saint Francis

e essence of prayer is intention, not attention

a. Toxic Grudges

"But if you do not forgive men their trespasses, neither will your Father forgive your trespasses."
Matt 6:15

Holding a grudge against someone is like trying to
harm him by taking poison a little at a time —
it harms me instead, without harming him.

The more I focus on a grudge,
the more its poison seeps into my soul,
and blocks my prayer.

Because grudges destroy my inner peace,
I will let go of them to preserve my peace within,
and to pray from my heart.

Letting go of grudges by focusing my attention on
the positive aspects of my life
also sets others at peace.

I will open my heart to forgive,
so my heart will be open
to receive God's forgiveness.

b. Difficult Grudges

Some difficult grudges from deep festering wounds are difficult to overcome because they are stored not only psychologically in the memory, but also physically in the body.

Healing from such grudges is a process that begins with an act of the will to forgive, a process that needs time to heal.

Once the decision to forgive is made, ("I do forgive this person.") the nasty thoughts and feelings of anger and hatred do not matter.

Whenever these nasty thoughts and angry feelings return, just pray: "God, I have already forgiven this person; I place the matter in your hands."

Repetition of this prayer will make the nasty thoughts and angry feelings return less often, and eventually fade away.

e essence of prayer is intention, not attention

Whenever these nasty thoughts and angry feelings return, just pray:

the essence of prayer is intention, not attentio

"God, I have already forgiven this person; I place the matter in your hands."

essence of prayer is intention, not attention

c. The Way of Forgiveness

"For if you forgive men their trespasses, your heavenly Father also will forgive you." Matt 6:14

If I refuse to forgive someone, the toxic resentment and grudge will poison my inner peace.

Forgiveness does not come from my feelings. Forgiveness does not come from my mind. Forgiveness comes from my will.

Once I have freely chosen to forgive someone by a decision of my will, the negative feelings and critical thoughts I have do not matter.

I will allow these natural negative feelings and critical thoughts to come and go.

Forgiving a person will open up my mind, heart, and spirit for receiving love from God and from others.

The way of forgiveness leads me to God Who is within me.

"Be kind to one another, compassionate, forgiving one another as God has forgiven you." Eph 4:32

the essence of prayer is intention, not attentic

d. Praying for My Foes

"You have heard it said, You shall love your neighbor and hate your enemy. But I say to you, love your enemies, pray for those who persecute you, that you may be children of your heavenly Father."
Matt 5:44-45

Because all emotions are good, I will learn to accept the negative emotions of others without becoming defensive.

I will learn to deflect criticisms or harsh words directed at me by not taking them in a personal way.

I will not descend to the muck of retaliation when I am offended or hurt by someone.

I will secretly calm myself with slow deep breathing and breathe in God's peace, when someone angry or upset confronts me.

I will secretly ask God to calm that person, and to grant that person peace.

e essence of prayer is intention, not attention

e. The Peace of Acceptance

"Bear one another's burdens, and so you will fulfill the law of Christ." Gal 6:2

Because the behavior of others is beyond my control,

I will stop trying to change other people.

Because I do not have access to the depths

of a person's emotional life or subconscious,

I will accept and respect people

without trying to understand them better.

Because love cannot be forced but must be freely given, I will accept the fact that I cannot make a person love me, or love me more.

Because I cannot make others happy,

I will create a loving atmosphere

wherein others can be happy

if they choose to be happy.

the essence of prayer is intention, not attention

Because God accepts me as I am, I will accept others as they are.

f. Bonding Through Prayer

"Let love be sincere; hate what is evil, hold on to what is good; love one another with mutual affection." Rom 12:9

Because I cannot change another person, to improve our relationship I will focus on changing myself.

To improve any of my relationships,
I have to change myself:

- my expectations

- my reactions and responses

- my attitudes

- my words and actions through daily prayer.

Because nagging begets resentment and resistance, I will limit the number of my kindly reminders.

Accepting others without pressuring them to change sets me at peace, and sets them at peace.

By receiving God's peace through daily prayer, I will become a channel of peace to others.

Preserving my peace within through prayer will make me easier to work with, and easier to live with.

By receiving
God's peace
through daily
prayer,
I will become
a channel of
peace to others.

essence of prayer is intention, not attention

g. Prayers of Love

"And this is my prayer: that your love may increase ever more and more in knowledge and every kind of perception, to discern what is of value, so that you may be pure and blameless for the day of Christ, filled with the fruit of righteousness that comes through Jesus Christ for glory and praise of God." Phil 1:9

The more I love others:

- the more I worry about them
- the more I suffer with them when they suffer
- the more I sacrifice for them
- the more vulnerable I become
- the more sensitive I become
- the more I pray for them.

Because God loves with an infinite love the ones I love, I will place them in God's loving care daily.

I will accept the negative emotions of anger, frustration, and disappointment that come with loving.

I will accept the negative thoughts and judgments that come with loving. Through prayer, God's love will cushion the lower lows that love brings me, and elevate the higher highs that come with loving.

the essence of prayer is intention, not attentia

Abbot John Chapman – with comments

- "God's presence in the soul is the life and nourishment of prayer."
- God within begins, sustains, and completes every prayer.
- "Pray as you can, and don't try to pray as you cannot."
- Simply pray in a way that is easiest for you in each situation.
- "Take yourself as you find yourself."
- That's the way God is taking you. Don't try to be what you are not in prayer. God is a God of reality, of the way things are.
- "The only way to pray is to pray; and the way to pray well is to pray much. The less one prays the worse it goes."

Praying much makes it easier to pray.

- "If you have no time to pray much at least pray regularly."

e essence of prayer is intention, not attention

- The best way to develop a good prayer life is with short frequent prayers scattered throughout the day: at rising, at bed time, before and after each meal, before each new task, when you or someone needs God's help, for a blessing or favor received.

- "If you must put up with the fact that when you do try to pray, you can't seem to get into it, then let your prayer consist of telling this to God." Father, (or Jesus or Holy Spirit) I'm having difficulty in praying; help me to pray.

- "Begin wherever you find yourself. Make any acts you want to make, but do not force yourself into feelings of any kind."

- Praying flows from the will, the intent, independently of how one is feeling.

- "If you don't know what to do when you have a quarter of an hour alone in church, then shut out everything else and just give yourself to God, and beg Him to have mercy on you, and offer Him all your distractions."

the essence of prayer is intention, not attentio

You could use this:

- As you inhale deeply and slowly you pray mentally –
"Lord Jesus Christ",
As you exhale slowly you pray mentally –
"Have mercy on us".

"Lord" means "God"

"Jesus" means "Savior"

"Christ" means "Anointed Priest"
(or Anointed Messiah")

"Have mercy" can mean "forgive" or "heal" or "help. "

"On us" includes family members, friends, and other persons.

e essence of prayer is intention, not attention

- "You can't get rid of the worries of this world or the questionings of the intellect, but you can laugh at them. Laugh at yourself and then think of God."

· Smile at them; or smile at yourself.

- "In the simple relation you have with God by prayer, it is as though you are in the center of a wheel where the noise of the revolving circumference does not matter."

- Place God at the center of your field of awareness. When you are distracted, return to God at the center of your field of awareness. This becomes easier with practice.

- "Pray in order to give yourself to God. Pure prayer is a prayer of the will; it is pure intention without words."

the essence of prayer is intention, not attentio

- Prayer is mainly a union of wills: a union of your will to God's will.

- St. Thomas Aquinas wrote,

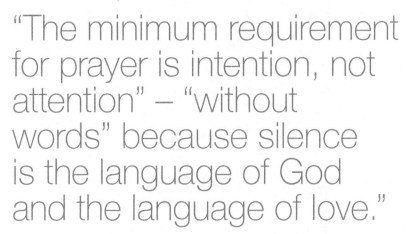

"The minimum requirement for prayer is intention, not attention" – "without words" because silence is the language of God and the language of love."

- Do not worry about what you should think or feel. Think about your intention to give yourself to God, cling to Him. Feelings are important for beginners, but they are not to be depended on. You do not have to reason that God is to be loved, except in the early stages. So do not worry about reasoning your way into God's presence.

essence of prayer is intention, not attention

Prayer transcends thoughts and feelings.
God is present within you,
loving you.

the essence of prayer is intention, not attentio

- "Want what He wants. Inner quiet is necessary for peace. But if God does not wish us to have peace we must be satisfied with confusion. So do not worry about reasoning your way into God's presence, which is peace of an elusive kind".

- God accepts us as we are.

- "If we prayed simply because we wanted the consolations of religion, the state of things would be very disappointing. But if we pray in order to give ourselves to God just as we are, then our imperfections at prayer at any given moment are what God wants. Granted it is not the very best we can do, but in general it is the only kind of prayer we can pray. Even if it is far from what we want, it is what God wants".

Pray just to be with God.

- "For those who love God all things work together toward the good. Every circumstance in life is a means to getting to heaven, and a part of God's Providence. So that at every moment we are in touch with God, including the times when we have feelings of distraction and are unable to pray peacefully".

e essence of prayer is intention, not attention

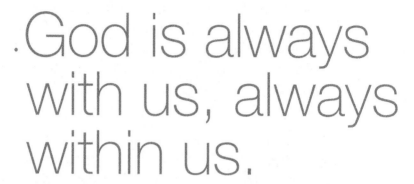

.God is always with us, always within us.

- "Minimize what happens in your own soul and maximize God's love for you. Do not think that distraction, dryness and desolation are merely stages of a trial which you pass through on your way to perfection. Perfection in this world is not a calm union with God, unless God so wishes. Jesus suffered temptation and desolation to show us that they are not incompatible with perfection, but in fact are part of perfection. Progress will be made when we become more and more indifferent as to what state we are in".

- Perfection on earth means doing your best with whatever you have, in whatever circumstances you're in. "Holy Acceptance" means accepting peacefully whatever God allows to happen.

the essence of prayer is intention, not attentio

- "Do not try to be simple, God does that for you. Your part is:
    - to think of others;
    - to be with God;
    - to avoid thinking about your own spiritual state."
- Simply praying means trying to focus only on God.
- "Simply be what God enables you to be at this moment. God is not only in every external event, but in every internal event, in every involuntary feeling you have — at every moment in your life you are in touch with God, and His hand is on you. You have only to be carried in His arms. Your one care must be not to jump free and try to walk alone; and finally when you are certain of His love, enjoy the Lord".

- During prayer, allow God to embrace you and love you.

essence of prayer is intention, not attention

- "You need not expect to be successful in these efforts. You need only to repeat that you want God's will. And if you must bear some form of suffering, physical, emotional or mental, do not get down on yourself. It is not against perfection to feel that suffering is intolerable, and it is all right to tell God that it is intolerable. Only try with the highest part of you to trust Him and be willing to suffer as long as He chooses, knowing that He will give you the necessary grace."

- No matter what you are experiencing, God loves you and will help you.

the essence of prayer is intention, not attentio

The Spirit of Freedom

- The Holy Spirit is the Spirit of Freedom because He is the Spirit of Truth that makes us free.

"I will ask the Father, and He will give you another Advocate, the Spirit of truth." John 14:16

"When the Spirit of truth comes, he will teach you all the truth." John 16:13

"You shall know the truth, and truth shall make you free." John 8:32

- The Spirit of Freedom guides and directs our praying. "But in like manner the Spirit also helps our weakness. For we do not know what we should pray for as we ought, but the Spirit himself pleads for us with unutterable groanings. And he who searches hearts knows what the Spirit desires, that he pleads for the saints according to God." Rom 8:26-7

- The Holy Spirit acts where it wills, and you "sense" its activity, but know not where it comes from or where it leads.

"The wind blows where it wills, and you hear its sound but know not where it comes from or where it goes." John 3:8

essence of prayer is intention, not attention

- With the Spirit of Freedom guiding and leading you, be free to:

- # pray any time you want;
- # pray anywhere you want;
- # pray any way you want.

- The Spirit of Freedom gives us the true freedom of Jesus Who was always "Yes" to the Father's will. "For the Son of God, Jesus Christ, … was not now 'Yes' and now 'No', but only 'Yes' was in him. For all the promises of God find their 'Yes' in him." 2nd Cor 1:19-20

the essence of prayer is intention, not attentio

The Jesus Prayer

Some think this form of prayer was probably made up by a monk in the 6th century at Mt. Sinai. Gregory of Sinai brought the prayer to Macedonia (Greece) in the 14th century. From there the prayer was brought to Russia in the 1800s, where it was practiced by many of the laity.

To do this form of prayer:

- Recollect (center) yourself by deep breathing.
- Use the breathing technique for relaxing by slowing your breathing rate and counting sets of 10.
- Then using a brief balanced prayer, synchronize the first half with inhalation and the second half with exhalation, while maintaining the same slow rate of breathing.
- When this process becomes semi-automatic, focus on the meaning of the words or the person you are addressing.

The traditional prayer used for this method was something like:

"Lord Jesus, Son of God, have mercy on me."

e essence of prayer is intention, not attention

We can also make up our own prayers to use for this method of praying by composing a short prayer of 10 - 14 syllables, and then divide the syllables into two equal parts. Here are examples:

"Lord Jesus, Son of Mary,

"Spirit of Jesus, please purify me.

"Jesus, Prince of Peace,

"Jesus, Light of the World,

"Jesus, Bread of Life,

"Jesus, Divine Physician,

"Heavenly Father,

"Our Mother of Sorrows,

"Blessed Mother,

the essence of prayer is intention, not attentio

- have mercy on me."

- (please grant me wisdom.)"

- please grant me Your peace."

- please enlighten my mind."

- please nourish my soul."

- please heal my mind, heart and soul."

- thank You for everything."

- please console and help them."

- teach me patience."

(Make up your own "Jesus Prayer")

e essence of prayer is intention, not attention

Two Zen Monks

In the middle ages in Japan, Two Zen monks left their monastery to beg for food and for alms in the village. They came to a wide shallow stream where a woman in a kimono and sandals could not cross it because of her attire.

The younger monk picked her up and carried her across the stream. She thanked him profusely.

On the way back from the village to the monastery, the older monk said, "You should not have carried her across the stream". [because of their vow of celibacy and chastity].

The younger monk replied, "Are you still carrying her? I left her at the stream long ago."

Detachment is mainly psychological. It avoids being preoccupied with a person, object, or activity.

Riddle: What is a Buddhist vacuum cleaner?
Answer: A vacuum without any attachments.

the essence of prayer is intention, not attentio

While visiting New York City, a devout Buddhist decided to try their famous Coney Island hot dog. Vendor: "What do you want on it?" Buddhist: "Make me one with everything." After handing the vendor a 20-dollar bill, he waits, and says, "Where's my change?" Vendor: "Change comes from within.

Question: Who was the best financier in the Bible?

Answer: The best financier in the Bible was Noah, Because he floated his assets while all the others went under.

essence of prayer is intention, not attention

Father Damien of Molokai

Fr. Damien served the lepers in Molokai, Hawaii, from 1873 to1889. During this time, he taught the Catholic faith to the lepers, cared for the patients himself, coordinated the building of houses, schools, roads, sanitary systems, hospitals, and a church.

After sixteen years of caring for the physical, emotional, and spiritual needs of those in the leper colony, Fr. Damien himself contracted leprosy. He continued with his work despite the infection, but finally died on April 15, 1889. The day of his passing, April 15, is a minor statewide holiday in Hawaii. He is the patron saint of the Diocese of Honolulu and of Hawaii.

Described as a "martyr of charity", Fr. Damien was canonized a saint by Pope Benedict XVI on October 11, 2009. The feast day of St. Damien is celebrated on May 10.

Despite the many obstacles he met and the many challenges he faced in his ministry, he continued because of his deep love for Christ and the lepers. His service was fueled by his profound prayer life. (Watch the movie "Molokai: The story of Fr. Damien)

the essence of prayer is intention, not attentic

Lectio Divina

Lectio

Lectio (reading): Listening as God speaks His words in Scripture. The Holy Spirit Who inspired the human authors of the N.T. is speaking these words within each of us here and now, according to the situation and needs of each person. Quiet the mind and heart to give full attention to God's external words and internal words. After centering oneself, slowly read and reread God's words with full attention, and allow the Holy Spirit within you to suggest personal thoughts and meanings. This part is non-analytical — do not analyze. Slowly repeat the word or phrase that strikes you.

Meditatio

Meditatio (meditation): God's words are multi-layered with multiple meanings. Through the guidance of the Holy Spirit, one layer tells us about God; another tells us about self; another tells me about my relationship with God; another tells me what God wants for me. This part is analytical. Seeking to understand the inspired words through the mind of Christ.

e essence of prayer is intention, not attention

Oratio

Oratio (prayer): My response to God's words with my words from the heart. Heart speaks to heart — a dialog between God's heart and your heart. Talking to God spontaneously from your heart. This spontaneous prayer arises from your pondering of the meanings of God's words.

Contemplatio

Contemplatio (contemplation): A non-analytical connection with God through simple awareness. Just focus on God intuitively. Being still — gazing at God — His smile shines — His love warms.

the essence of prayer is intention, not attentio

The foundation of prayer is Divine Revelation/ Scripture. Scripture can be used as a foundation for prayer. What is greater than my desire to pray? God's desire that I pray.

Prayer is primarily my response to God inviting me to converse with Him.

Thoughts from St. John of the Cross: "The human person is a mystery of emptiness; God is a mystery of infinite fullness." His thoughts on Luke 11:9: "Seek in Reading Scripture, and you will find in Meditation; knock in Prayer, and it will be opened to you in Contemplation."

Dom Marmion:

- "We read Scripture (lectio)
- with the eyes of God (meditatio)
- until the heart is touched (oratio)
- and leaps to flame (contemplatio)."

What are the foundations of Christianity and our spiritual life? God sees me exactly as I am with all my flaws, selfishness, sins, and weaknesses, and yet accepts and loves me unconditionally as I am.

essence of prayer is intention, not attention

What is the path to complete reliance on God? Our failures along that path. What does it mean to accept God's unconditional love, unconditionally? How do we do this? To share in the life of Jesus through the Holy Spirit is to share in His prayer life, contemplation, and ministry.

• "Tradere aliis contemplata."
‒ to share with others the fruits of your contemplation.

• Lectio Divina
- is a flow, so we need to be fluid. "Be like water."

• Lectio Divina
- involves all our faculties and powers. Prayer is done in the context of my daily living.

the essence of prayer is intention, not attentio

The Sacred Liturgy as the Mystery of our Redemption

The Sacred Liturgy includes the Sacrifice of the Mass, the Sacraments, and the praying of the Divine Office, also known as the Liturgy of Hours.

The Eucharistic Sacrifice of the Mass includes Holy Communion and the Real Presence of the Risen Christ in the Blessed Sacrament.

The Sacrifice of the Mass is the re-presentation of Jesus' actual sacrifice of love and thanks on the cross at Calvary in a sacramental manner.

Only one Sacrifice of Jesus, but many, many Masses.

essence of prayer is intention, not attention

The Sacred Liturgy is the continuation and extension of the ongoing redeeming activity of the Risen Christ across time and space.

- Plus: The redeeming power of His suffering, death, resurrection, and prayers flows to us through the Mass, Sacraments, and Liturgy of Hours.

- Plus: Everyday, millions of Masses are being offered throughout the world. Because of the various time zones, the Sacrifice of the Mass is being offered continually somewhere in the world.

- Plus: Everyday, millions of people are receiving Holy Communion throughout the world.

- Plus: Everyday, millions of priests, religious, and lay persons are praying the Liturgy of Hours. Because of the various time zones, the Liturgy of Hours is being prayed continually throughout the day.

- Plus: Everyday, Sacraments are being administered to people somewhere in the world continually.

the essence of prayer is intention, not attentio

So the Sacred Liturgy is the continuation and extension of the ongoing redeeming activity of the Risen Christ across time and space.

It is the Risen Christ Who offers every Mass, and administers every Sacrament. Human persons serve as His instruments.

There are nine Sacraments in all:

The Primary Sacrament is the Person of the Risen Christ. The Fundamental Sacrament is the Church, His Mystical Body. There are seven Liturgical Sacraments – Baptism, Confirmation, Confession, the Mass, Anointing of the sick, Holy Orders, and Matrimony.

The Risen Christ administers every Liturgical Sacrament in and through the Church, His Mystical Body. Just as the Sacred Liturgy is the continuation and extension of the ongoing redeeming activity of the Risen Christ across time and space, so too, The Church, His Mystical Body, is the continuation and extension of the Person of the Risen Christ through time and space.

e essence of prayer is intention, not attention

Everything described here is like the magnetic field around the earth which forms an invisible "shield" encasing the earth. This magnetic field around the earth makes all life possible on our earth because it:

- keeps in our atmosphere around the earth - without it, our atmosphere would drift off into space;

- protects our earth from radiation from solar flares and from cosmic rays, which are lethal to all forms of life; yet

- lets in sunlight so necessary for life on earth;

- Keeps in the ozone layer which protects all life from lethal UV light.

- gives us both magnetic poles which make navigation possible for animals and for us.

Whenever we take part in the Sacrifice of the Mass, or in a Sacrament, or pray the liturgy of Hours, we contribute to the redeeming activity of the Risen Christ as His collaborators.

the essence of prayer is intention, not attentio

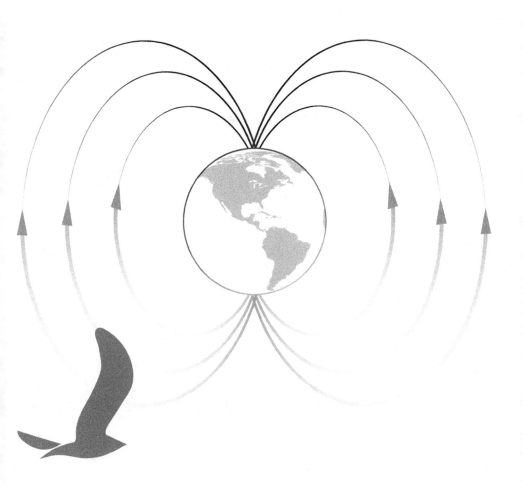

e essence of prayer is intention, not attention

Prayer of Saint Francis

Lord, make me an instrument of your peace:
where there is hatred, let me sow love;
where there is injury, pardon;
where there is doubt, faith;
where there is despair, hope;
where there is darkness, light;
where there is sadness, joy.

O divine Master, grant that I may not so much seek
to be consoled as to console,
to be understood as to understand,
to be loved as to love.
For it is in giving that we receive,
it is in pardoning that we are pardoned,
and it is in dying that we are born to eternal life.

Amen.

the essence of prayer is intention, not attentio

essence of prayer is intention, not attention

Ⓑ The Gifts of the Holy Spirit for Prayer

a. Knowledge
b. Understanding
c. Wisdom
d. Counsel
e. Fear of the Lord
f. Piety
g. Fortitude

the essence of prayer is intention, not attenti...

a. Knowledge

Jesus gave us the Holy Spirit to be our constant guide and teacher. The Holy Spirit teaches us about the spiritual life and about prayer.

In prayer He teaches us about the Father, about Jesus, about Himself.

In prayer He teaches us about ourselves and about our relationships.

He guides and helps our praying.

He gives us knowledge about many things.

b. Understanding

We know many things without understanding them fully.

During prayer the Holy Spirit gives us a better understanding of many things.

He gives us insights about the Father, Jesus, and Himself.

He gives us a deeper understanding of self and of others.

He helps us to understand the connections between persons and between things and reality.

c. Wisdom

Wisdom is the ability to "see" the whole picture and all the parts and their place in order of importance.

This a special ability that few have. Many know a lot of facts but lack wisdom.

Sacred Scripture praises wisdom, especially in the spiritual life.

The Gift of Wisdom from the Holy Spirit helps a person to "see" the whole picture and the relations between God, persons, things and events.

This Wisdom is directly connected to the Charity, the ability to love as God loves (forever and unconditionally).

Regular prayer leads to Wisdom.

d. Counsel

Counsel, similar to the virtue of prudence, is the ability to apply knowledge, understanding, wisdom to definite decisions in specific circumstances.

We make many, many decisions every day. Some are good, some are better, and some are best. Some are bad, some are worse, and some are worst.

"Good, better, best. Never let it rest, till the good is better, and the better best." An excellent motto for the spiritual life and prayer life.

Seek Counsel from the Holy Spirit in prayer for your daily decisions.

e. Fear of the Lord

This Gift of the Holy Spirit means a profound respect for God, that never takes God for granted.

Most people take God for granted and seldom think of Him.

Praying links your life to God's life.

Prayer deepens your respect for God, and your appreciation of God.

Through prayer, your fear of offending God grows.

f. Piety

Piety means respecting and loving God our Father, as the best of all fathers.

This respect for God our Father is expressed by obeying His commands.

This love for God our Father is expressed by our service to others.

Praying deepens our respect for God our Father.

Prayer strengthens our love for God our Father, and for others.

g. Fortitude

Fortitude is the inner strength – psychological and spiritual – for living out our Christian vocation with fidelity, despite the challenge and obstacles.

All the Saints had fortitude because of their prayer life, especially the martyrs.

They encouraged Christians to gather inner strength from a life of prayer.

We need to keep asking God for help through prayer whenever we need help.

We need prayer to help us "bounce" when challenges and obstacles get us "down", discouraged.

ⓒ Resources for Reflection

1. God is the maker, giver, and keeper of time.
2. Focus on your weaknesses and on God's Love and Goodness.

   "When I am weak then I am strong."
   2 Cor 12:10

3. Prayer and contemplation destroy the root of sin: they make God (instead of self) the center of your life.
4. All virtues are found in prayer and contemplation (God).
5. God starts, sustains, and perfects prayer and contemplation.

Prayer follows God

the essence of prayer is intention, not attentio

6. Let God deal with you as He wants.
   Let the Holy Spirit act within you and through you.

7. A short intense prayer penetrates heaven
   like a bullet.

8. Prayer and contemplation are different for each
   person; its path and experience.

9. You don't have to express your desires to
   God all the time – He knows.

10. In liturgical prayer the body leads the spirit;
    but in contemplation the spirit leads the body.

Prayer simplifies

e essence of prayer is intention, not attention

11. St. Bernard: "Perfect humility has no limits."
12. Keep focusing on God alone.
13. Our cross is the burden of self-awareness.
14. Our mind is an ongoing endless maze, labyrinth; Christ is the Door to prayer and contemplation.
15. Without Me you can do nothing. God starts, sustains, and completes prayer and contemplation.

Prayer energizes

the essence of prayer is intention, not attentio

16. In the Old Testament clouds symbolize liberation, and God's love and loyalty.

17. St. Teresa of Avila: "4 ways to water a garden (of prayer):"

  a "draw water from a well"

  b "use a water wheel to pour water onto a trough near or in the garden"

  c "irrigate from a stream running through the garden"

  d "let it rain"

18. God plays "hide and seek" with us.

19. The painful process of purification goes from sensations to spiritual experience to spiritual understanding to being "touched" by God.

20. "St. Bernard: From the Word make flesh to the Word as Wisdom to the Word as Holiness."

Prayer resets our sight

essence of prayer is intention, not attention

21. Rule of St.Benedict: "Ora et Labora"
    + "Lectio Divina" + "Liturgy"

22. "Hesychia" means the quiet prayer of the heart.

23. St. Gregory of Palamas:
    "Mary is the perfect hesychast."

24. The "Jesus Prayer" (very incarnational):
    This is done in a state of quiet without reading,
    thinking, reasoning, or imagining.

    Repeat with faith and love this "Jesus Prayer":
    Lord, Jesus Christ (with inhalation)
    Have mercy on us (with exhalation)

    Synchronize this prayer with your breathing
    while focusing on your heart.

    A light or warmth may or may not be apparent.

    The result is "theosis" (deification) — becoming
    God-like.

25. In the 19th c. a Russian was instructed to use
    the "Jesus Prayer" wherever he went, and wrote
    "The Way of a Pilgrim" — this practice led to
    inner peace and compassion for all the people
    he met. The "Jesus Prayer" can become a
    murmuring of the heart.

the essence of prayer is intention, not attentio

Prayer transforms

26. The great Russian mystic Theophan the Recluse retired as bishop to live in solitude for prayer and for writing letters of spiritual direction. He said the "Jesus Prayer" enkindles a flame of love in the heart. He died in 1359 and was canonized in 1368.

27. God Who is inaccessible in His essence is present in His energies (activities). He is wholly unknowable in His essence, yet revealed in His energies (activities). God is tremendous energy, which overflows onto the senses and causes intense delight or acute suffering.

28. The Whole Christ is the Cosmic Christ.

"The Father and I are one." John. 10:30

29. St.Teresa: "For mental prayer in my opinion is nothing else than an intimate sharing between friends; it means taking time frequently to be alone with Him Who we know loves us." (Life 8:4)

30. Vat. II — The union between human persons is modelled on the union between the Persons of the Holy Trinity.

the essence of prayer is intention, not attentio

Prayer unifies

essence of prayer is intention, not attention

31. John. 17:21 "That they may be one as I, Father, in you and you in me, that they may one in us."

32. Being with God, the Center of the Cosmos, Who is radiating His healing, transforming love.

33. St. Ignatius: "God's presence is constant because you can find God in all things."

34. Conversion: intellectual, ethical, religious. Unrestricted love is the heart of all authentic religious experience in all the great Religions. Religions differ in outer beliefs, but can be deeply united in faith.

    Being in love means the beloved and I are in each other.

    • Outer belief is the superstructure in history and conditioned by culture.

    • Inner faith is the infrastructure from the inner light from God. This inner light leads to outer revelation and is nourished by its revelation.

35. Be nothing so God can be your Everything.

36. The path of purification from sin and sinful inclinations is a path of liberation — this lasts till death. This purification and liberation come from Christ's passion and Resurrection.

the essence of prayer is intention, not attentio

Prayer expands one's soul

St. Augustine: He addresses the soul, "I did not find you without, Lord, because I wrongly sought you without, who were within." And he addresses the soul, telling her of the wonderful riches that are within where the Beloved dwells; "What more do you want, O soul! And what else do you search for outside, when

within yourself you possess your riches,

delights, satisfactions, fullness and kingdom — your Beloved whom you desire and seek?"

the essence of prayer is intention, not attentio

Be joyful and glad in your interior recollection with him, for you have him so close to you. Desire him there, adore him there.

Do not go in pursuit of him outside yourself.

You will only become distracted and wearied thereby, and you shall not find him, or enjoy him more securely, or sooner, or more intimately that by seeking him within you.

e essence of prayer is intention, not attention

Needless to say, this doctrine is found throughout the fourth gospel as in the words of Jesus: "Those who love me will keep my word, and my Father will love them, and we will come to them and make our home with them". (John 14:23)

Holy Spirit, divine Spirit of light and love, I consecrate to you my mind, heart, and will for time and for eternity. May my understanding be always submissive to your inspiration. Inflame my heart with love for God and for others. Conform my will to your will. Help me to relive the life and virtues of Jesus - his purity, humility, and charity – to whom with the Father and you be glory forever.

Amen.

the essence of prayer is intention, not attentio

Holy Spirit,

may your plans be my plans;
may your ways be my ways;
may your will be my will;
may your time be my time.
Amen.

essence of prayer is intention, not attention

Part 3
ARRIVING

As you read,
as you learn
to pray, as you
go through life,
above you the
Holy Spirit will
always be there
to help

Holy Spirit

You

The essence
of prayer is
intention,
not affection.

the essence of prayer is intention, not attentio

It's important that you pray often and regularly, but it doesn't matter how you pray.

essence of prayer is intention, not attention

Prayer is union with God, being with God.

Praying is like being in a small sailboat with God steering and the Holy Spirit blowing it along.

essence of prayer is intention, not attention

The following factors do not change the reality
of your being with God, your praying:

- smooth, choppy, or stormy sea;
  (your state of mind and/or emotional state)

- calm, changing, or blustery winds;
  (your situation and/or circumstances of life)

- various sea birds or creatures coming or going;
  (the distractions that come and go)

- whether you're alert or not, comfortable or not,
  fearful or not; (your physical-psychological state)

- whether you're talking to God or just being silent.

You are praying because you are with God.
God accepts you as you are, no matter your situation
or your circumstances.

the essence of prayer is intention, not attentio

While praying:

- Whether your state of mind or emotional state is smooth, choppy, or stormy does not matter.

- Whether your present situation or circumstances of life is calm, changing, or blustery does not matter.

- Whether few or many distractions come or go does not matter.

- Whether you're alert or drowsy, with comfort, discomfort or pain, fearful or calm does not matter.

e essence of prayer is intention, not attention

The Heart of Prayerfulness

The heart of prayerfulness is the heart of Christ's prayer life. The heart of Christ's prayer life is His love for the Father and for us. Jesus prayed from His heart guided by the Holy Spirit. How do we enter into this heart of His prayer life? We enter into the heart of Christ's prayer life through the Holy Spirit, Who is the Bond of Love between Jesus and the Father, and between Jesus and us. By being with the Holy Spirit and following His guidance, we are led into the heart of Christ's prayer life, the heart of prayerfulness. Praying from the heart means praying with love, praying with the Holy Spirit.

the essence of prayer is intention, not attentio

The Prayer of Jesus for Oneness

"In that day you will know that I am in my Father, and you in me, and I in you." John 14:20

What we long for is oneness with Christ and the experience of oneness with God as Unitive Love.

"that all may be one, even as thou, Father, in me and I in thee, that they also may be one in us." John 17:21

This is the Oneness of the 3 Divine Persons as One God; each Person living with each Other, and in each Other, and for each Other.

We can become one with the 3 Divine Persons, And one with the One God.

"He, however, who drinks of this water that I will give him shall never thirst; but the water that I shall give him shall become in him a fountain of water, springing up unto life everlasting." John 4:14

We need to enter into God's Kingdom of His unitive Trinitarian Love, into the I AM Trinitarian Life flow of the Divine Indwelling. Through contemplation you move your emotions, thoughts, and heart into God's Kingdom of unitive Trinitarian Love.

e essence of prayer is intention, not attention

Silent contemplation experiences the goodness and beauty of God in a wordless way.

Sacred Silence

Silence = stillness + awareness

the essence of prayer is intention, not attentio

St. John of the Cross : "The Father spoke His Word, His Son, in eternal silence, and He must be heard in silence." "The entire universe is a sea of love in which one is engulfed." (Sponge) God's love flows around us and within us. God is Love outpouring itself.

What are we?
We are God's love outpoured.

Separation from God is an illusion.
True or False

True. God is more around me and more within me than the ocean is around a sponge and within this sponge at the bottom of the ocean.

St. Theophan the Recluse: "Descend from your head to your heart." You are not your thoughts nor your feelings, but the underlying spirit deep within you that is aware of these thoughts and feelings. (You are the mountain, not the changing weather.) Breathing into Silent Stillness (God). The Silence that is God is alive and liberating. The pathless path to prayer is the present moment. God is always Self-giving.

With the guidance of the Holy Spirit, go from the mechanical to the psychological to the spiritual to the Divine Indwelling. The prayer words (or word) draw all our thoughts and feelings into a unifying point without thoughts and feelings.

Words --- word --- silence --- just being with God.

Awareness is the eyes of silence. God is fully aware of me. When I am fully aware of God, the union of my awareness of God with God's awareness of me is like the union of two lights. Distractions hone our skill for centering. Acknowledge them with stillness and then refocus. The entrance into God's Silence is the wound outside the heart of Jesus. He joins His wounds to our wounds (sin, failure, disgrace, brokenness) to heal us. Are the wounds of Jesus shameful? He has placed our wounds in His wounds.

the essence of prayer is intention, not attentio

My silence ──────────▶
  Silence Itself

My awareness ──────────▶
  Awareness Itself

My solitude (psychological
and spiritual) ──────────▶
  Divine Solidarity

(One God with Three Divine Persons)

e essence of prayer is intention, not attention

the essence of prayer is intention, not attentio

A The Radiance of God Within

"May the God of hope fill you with all joy and peace in believing, so that you may abound in hope by the power of the Holy Spirit." Rom 15:13

a. God's Peace

b. God's Light

c. God's Wisdom

d. God's Strength

e. God's Love

a. God's Peace

"May the Lord of peace himself give you peace at all times and in every way." 2 Thes 3:16

Whenever the need arises -- at home, at work, or elsewhere I will use the following prayer:

As I inhale slowly and deeply, mentally I say, "I breathe in God's peace,"

As I exhale slowly, mentally I say, "I breathe out tension."

Or

As I inhale slowly and deeply, mentally I say, "I breathe in God's peace,"

As I exhale slowly, mentally I say, "I breathe out worry."

After doing this for three or five minutes, I will be calm, clear, and centered with God's peace.

As I calm my inner self and breathe in God's peace, God will envelop me with the embrace of His peace.

b. God's Light

"For you were once darkness, but now you are light in the Lord. Live as children of light, for light produces every kind of good works." Eph 5:8-9

Whenever the need arises — at home, at work, or elsewhere — I will use the following prayer:

As I inhale slowly and deeply, mentally I say, "I breathe in God's light;"

As I exhale slowly, mentally I say, "I breathe out darkness."

or

As I inhale slowly and deeply, mentally I say, "I breathe in God's light,"

As I exhale slowly, mentally I say, "I breathe out my gloom."

After doing this for three or five minutes, I will have the brightness and clarity of God's light.

As I calm my inner self and breathe in God's light, God will envelop me with the radiance of His light.

essence of prayer is intention, not attention

"I am the Light

of the world"

John 8:12

e essence of prayer is intention, not attention

c. God's Wisdom

"All wisdom comes from God and is with him forever." Sirach 1:1

Whenever the need arises — at home, at work, or elsewhere — I will use the following prayer:

As I inhale slowly and deeply, mentally I say, "I breathe in God's wisdom;"

As I exhale slowly, mentally I say, "I breathe out confusion."

or

As I inhale slowly and deeply, mentally I say, "I breathe in God's wisdom;"

As I exhale slowly, mentally I say, "I breathe out ignorance."

After doing this for three or five minutes, I will be calm, clear, and guided by God's wisdom.

As I calm my inner self and breathe in God's wisdom, I will be more open to God's wisdom and guidance.

"For wisdom is better than jewels, and all that you may desire cannot compare with her." Prov 8:11

the essence of prayer is intention, not attentio

d. God's Strength

"The Almighty — we cannot find him; he is great in power and justice, righteousness he will not violate." Job 37:23

Whenever the need arises — at home, at work, or elsewhere — I will use the following prayer:

As I inhale slowly and deeply, mentally I say, "I breathe in God's strength;"

As I exhale slowly, mentally I say, "I breathe out fatigue."

Or

As I inhale slowly and deeply, mentally I say, "I breathe in God's strength;"

As I exhale slowly, mentally I say, "I breathe out weakness."

After doing this for three or five minutes, I will be stronger with God's strength. As I calm my inner self and breathe in God's strength, He will strengthen my heart and soul.

essence of prayer is intention, not attention

e. God's Love

*"I have loved you with an everlasting love;
Therefore, I have continued my faithfulness
to you." Jer 31:3*

Because God is within me, at the center
of my soul, with His immense love for me,
I am surrounded by His love.

As I inhale slowly and deeply, mentally I say,
"I breathe in God's love;"

As I exhale slowly, mentally I say
"I breathe out anger."

or

As I inhale slowly and deeply, mentally I say,
"I breathe in God's love;"

As I exhale slowly, mentally I say,
"I breathe out frustration."

or

As I inhale slowly and deeply, mentally I say,
"I breathe in God's love;"

As I exhale slowly, mentally I say,
"I breathe out loneliness."

As I calm my inner self and breathe in God's love,
God will embrace me with the warmth of His love.

the essence of prayer is intention, not attentio

B Radiance with God's Brightness

a. Being Still

b. APT Living for God

c. Flowing with God

d. A Channel of God's peace

e. God is Love

f. God Within Me

g. The Guest Within

h. Come, Holy Spirit

i. Receiving God's Goodness

j. God's Gifts

Gift 1 – God's Light

Gift 2 - God's Wisdom

Gift 3 – God's Strength

Gift 4 – God's Love

Gift 5 – God's Truth and Justice

Gift 6 – God's Joy and Purity

Gift 7 – God's Beauty

"Lower a bucket" – a true story

essence of prayer is intention, not attention

a. Being Still

"Be still, and know that I am God." Psalm 46:10

Through prayer, I will transform daily stress into a power-source for my commitment to my loved ones, and the challenge of my own growth and development.

With my regular nightly practice of relaxing my body and calming my inner self before getting into bed, I will be still enough to experience my inner peace, and fall asleep in God's arms.

With my daily use of the slow deep breathing technique, I will be calm, clear, and centered with God's peace.

I will use relaxation techniques daily to calm my mind, emotions, and heart, to find and experience God within me.

Because the only obstacle to finding God in and through prayer is myself, by not praying, I will pray daily and often.

the essence of prayer is intention, not attentic

b. APT Living for God

"He has showed you, O man, what is good; and what does the Lord require of you but to do justice, and to love kindness, and to walk humbly with your God." Micah 6:8

I will be like the wise sailor of a sail boat in choppy seas, who makes full use of all that is within his control, with total trust in God, instead of focusing on the forces of the wind and waves that are beyond his control.

Because everything I do affects and forms my thoughts, feelings, and character, I will focus on fulfilling my daily tasks well and with inner calmness, for God and for others.

APT living:

Acceptance of my present situation with
Purpose in mind for doing well the
Task at hand —

will create the aptitude for:

- doing quality work,
- relating well with others,
- enjoying my life more fully,
- and being a channel of God's blessings to others.

I will shape and transform myself into a patient, reliable, loving person through APT living, and through daily prayer.

e essence of prayer is intention, not attention

c. Flowing with God

"In him we live and move and have our being."
Acts 17:28

Because daily changes are continuous in my life,
I will flow with these changes like water, and work
with them, while directing my flow toward my
spiritual goals.

I will let go of the past and the future to flow with
the present, so I can deal with what's real and
beneficial, because God is " I AM".

I will flow around the big rocks (things beyond my
control) by accepting or ignoring them, while trusting
in God's love for me.

I will preserve the peace within the center of my soul,
as I flow with changes up and down, side to side,
while knowing God is always within me.

Because God cares about everything in my life,
I will talk to God about anything and everything.

the essence of prayer is intention, not attentio

I will let go of the past
and the future to flow
with the present,
so I can deal with
what's real and
beneficial, because
God is...

"I AM"

essence of prayer is intention, not attention

d. A Channel of God's Peace

"Lord, make me a channel of Your peace."
St. Francis of Assisi

Because of God's love for everyone, I will accept and show respect to everyone, to set others at peace.

Because God's forgiveness awaits me, I will let go of grudges and resentment, for internal peace and external peace.

Because God's love is within me, I will channel my flow of patience and kindness to lead others to inner peace.

Because I am a channel of God's peace, I will reassure and encourage others with my kind, supportive words, to allow God's peace to flow out to others.

Because praying will transform me into a patient, loving person, I will pray daily and often.

Because our loving God answers every prayer with a positive response, I will pray for others and for self with total trust and confidence.

the essence of prayer is intention, not attentio

e. God is Love

"In him was life, and the life was the light of men. The light shines in the darkness, and the darkness has not overcome it." John 1:4-5

"He who does not love does not know God; for God is love." 1 John 4:8

Because God is my Life, Light, and Love, I will draw from His life, light, and love, present at the center of my soul.

Because God is omniscient (all-knowing) and omnipotent (all-powerful), He knows what's best for me and can help me, I will accept whatever He allows to happen to me.

Because God is verified by His goodness and beauty in His creation, I will strive to link all goodness and beauty with God's Goodness and Beauty.

Because God is everywhere, in myself and in others, I will show respect to God in others and in myself.

essence of prayer is intention, not attention

f. God Within Me

"Do you not know that you are the temple of God, and that the Spirit of God dwells in you?" I Cor 3:16

Because God is within me, at the center of my soul, I will seek Him within myself through prayer.

Because God is found in the midst of peace, I will calm my inner self with slow deep breathing before praying.

Because God within awaits and welcomes me, I will seek Him within myself through prayer often, anywhere, and anytime.

Because God within loves everyone, I will let His love flow out from me to everyone.

the essence of prayer is intention, not attentio

g. The Guest Within

"In the same way the Spirit too comes to the aid of our weakness; for we do not know how to pray as we ought, but the Spirit itself intercedes with inexpressible groanings." Rom 8:26

e essence of prayer is intention, not attention

h. Come, Holy Spirit

Replace the tension within us
with a holy relaxation.

Replace the turbulence within
us with a sacred calm.

Replace the anxiety within us
with a quiet confidence.

Replace the fear within us
with a strong faith.

Replace the bitterness within us
with the sweetness of grace.

Replace the darkness within us
with a gentle light.

Replace the coldness within us
with a loving warmth .

Replace the night within us
with Your day.

Replace the winter within us
with Your spring.

Straighten our crookedness,
fill our emptiness.

the essence of prayer is intention, not attentio

Dull the edge of our pride, smooth the flow of our humbleness. Illumine the light of our love, quench the flames of our lust. Let us see ourselves as You see us, that we may see You as You have promised, and be fortunate according to Your word: "Blessed are the pure of heart, for they shall see God." Amen

essence of prayer is intention, not attention

i. Receiving God's Goodness

"Let nothing disturb you; nothing cause you fear; all things pass. God is unchanging. Patience obtains all; whoever has God needs nothing else. God alone suffices." (Bookmark of St. Teresa of Avila)

Through prayer, my union with God within me will:

- heal the wounds of my past pains
- purify me of arrogance and selfishness
- increase my inner strength and courage
- teach me patience and endurance
- deepen my faith and trust in God
- give me peace of mind, peace of heart, and peace of soul
- expand my love for God and for others.

Through daily prayer, I will go to God within me:

- to seek help for others and for self
- to seek refuge in times of trouble
- to receive God's gifts and blessings
- to enjoy the spiritual peace He gives
- to share in God's life, light, and love

"How great is your goodness, O Lord, which you have in store for those who fear you." Psalm 31:20

the essence of prayer is intention, not attentio

j. God's Gifts

"For this very reason, make every effort to add to your faith goodness; and to goodness, knowledge; and to knowledge, self-control; and to self-control, perseverance; and to perseverance, godliness; and to godliness, mutual affection; and to mutual affection, love." 2 Peter 1:5-7

Gift 1 - God's Light

Gift 2 - God's Wisdom

Gift 3 - God's Strength

Gift 4 - God's Love

Gift 5 - God's Truth and Justice

Gift 6 - God's Joy and Purity

Gift 7 - God's Beauty

essence of prayer is intention, not attention

Gift 1 - God's Light

As I inhale slowly and deeply, mentally I say,
"I breathe in God's light;"

As I exhale slowly, mentally I say,
"I breathe out darkness."

As I inhale slowly and deeply, mentally I say,
"I breathe in God's light;"

As I exhale slowly, mentally I say,
"I breathe out sadness."

As I inhale slowly and deeply, mentally I say,
"I breathe in God's light;"

As I exhale slowly, mentally I say,
"I breathe out my gloom."

As I inhale slowly and deeply, mentally I say,
"I breathe in God's light;"

As I exhale slowly, mentally I say,
"I breathe out blindness."

the essence of prayer is intention, not attentio

Gift 2 - God's Wisdom

As I inhale slowly and deeply, mentally I say,
"I breathe in God's wisdom;"

As I exhale slowly, mentally I say,
"I breathe out confusion."

As I inhale slowly and deeply, mentally I say,
"I breathe in God's wisdom;"

As I exhale slowly, mentally I say,
"I breathe out ignorance."

As I inhale slowly and deeply, mentally I say,
"I breathe in God's wisdom;"

As I exhale slowly, mentally I say,
"I breathe out helpful words."

As I inhale slowly and deeply, mentally I say,
"I breathe in God's wisdom;"

As I exhale slowly, mentally I say,
"I breathe out stupidity."

The essence of prayer is intention, not attention

Gift 3 - God's Strength

As I inhale slowly and deeply, mentally I say,
"I breathe in God's strength;"

As I exhale slowly, mentally I say,
"I breathe out weakness."

As I inhale slowly and deeply, mentally I say,
"I breathe in God's strength;"

As I exhale slowly, mentally I say,
"I breathe out fatigue."

As I inhale slowly and deeply, mentally I say,
"I breathe in God's power;"

As I exhale slowly, mentally I say,
"I breathe out helplessness."

As I inhale slowly and deeply, mentally I say,
"I breathe in God's power;"

As I exhale slowly, mentally I say,
"I breathe out cowardice."

the essence of prayer is intention, not attentio

Gift 4 - God's Love

As I breathe in slowly and deeply, mentally I say,
"I breathe in God's love;"

As I breathe out slowly and deeply, mentally I say,
"I breathe out anger."

As I inhale slowly and deeply, mentally I say,
"I breathe in God's love;"

As I exhale slowly, mentally I say,
"I breathe out frustration."

As I inhale slowly and deeply, mentally I say,
"I breathe in God's love;"

As I exhale slowly, mentally I say,
"I breathe out loneliness."

As I inhale slowly and deeply, mentally I say,
"I breathe in God's love;"

As I exhale slowly, mentally I say,
"I breathe out restlessness."

essence of prayer is intention, not attention

As I inhale slowly and deeply, mentally I say,
I breathe in God's love;

As I exhale slowly, mentally I say,
"I breathe out emptiness."

As I inhale slowly and deeply, mentally I say,
"I breathe in God's love;"

As I exhale slowly, mentally I say,
"I breathe out selfishness."

As I inhale slowly and deeply, mentally I say,
"I breathe in God's love;"

As I exhale slowly, mentally I say,
"I breathe out anguish."

the essence of prayer is intention, not attentio

Gift 5 - God's Truth and Justice

As I inhale slowly and deeply, mentally I say,
"I breathe in Gods truth;"

As I exhale slowly, mentally I say,
"I breathe out deceit."

As I inhale slowly and deeply, mentally I say,
"I breathe in God's truth;"

As I exhale slowly, mentally I say,
"I breathe out lying."

As I inhale slowly and deeply, mentally I say,
"I breathe in God's justice;"

As I exhale slowly, mentally I say,
"I breathe out injustice."

As I inhale slowly and deeply, mentally I say,
"I breathe in God's justice;"

As I exhale slowly, mentally I say,
"I breathe out unfairness."

As I inhale slowly and deeply, mentally I say,
"I breathe in God's humbleness;"

As I exhale slowly, mentally I say,
"I breathe out arrogance and pride."

essence of prayer is intention, not attention

Gift 6 - God's Joy and Purity

As I inhale slowly and deeply, mentally I say,
"I breathe in God's joy;"

As I exhale slowly, mentally I say,
"I breathe out sadness."

As I inhale slowly and deeply, mentally I say,
"I breathe in God's joy and peace;"

As I exhale slowly, mentally I say,
"I breathe out disappointment."

As I inhale slowly and deeply, mentally I say,
"I breathe in God's purity;"

As I exhale slowly, mentally I say,
"I breathe out impurity."

As I inhale slowly and deeply, mentally I say,
"I breathe in God's purity;"

As I exhale slowly, mentally I say,
"I breathe out negativity."

the essence of prayer is intention, not attentio

Gift 7 - God's Beauty

As I inhale slowly and deeply, mentally I say,
"I breathe in God's beauty;"

As I exhale slowly, mentally I say,
"I breathe out disorder."

As I inhale slowly and deeply, mentally I say,
"I breathe in God's beauty;"

As I exhale slowly, mentally I say,
"I breathe out ugliness."

As I inhale slowly and deeply, mentally I say,
"I breathe in God's creativeness;"

As I exhale slowly, mentally I say,
"I breathe out my dullness."

As I inhale slowly and deeply, mentally I say,
"I breathe in God's creativeness;"

As I exhale slowly, mentally I say,
"I breathe out my blandness."

e essence of prayer is intention, not attention

"Lower a Bucket" - a true story

In the early 1800's a large sailing ship was stranded off the coast of South America for three days by a dead calm. The captain had dropped anchor to prevent the waves from pushing the ship to the rocks off shore. Even if the wind returned, it would take two or three days to find a port with fresh water.

A large steam ship was passing nearby, so the captain raised the megaphone to his mouth and shouted, "Help! Help! We are stranded and need drinking water." The captain of the steam ship shouted back, "Lower a bucket! Lower a bucket!"

"This is no joking matter! We are desperate for drinking water!" (Drinking salt water would make a person even thirstier, and could kill him.) As the steam ship went away, its captain shouted, "Lower a bucket! Lower a bucket!" In despair, the captain went down to his cabin. A deck hand who heard all of this lowered a bucket to taste the water. Fresh water! The ship was off the mouth of the Amazon River and millions of gallons of fresh water were flowing to the ocean.

the essence of prayer is intention, not attentio

Millions of people are thirsting for true love. Yet they are floating on the ocean of God's Love. You are a sea sponge at the bottom of the ocean. You look around. What do you see? You look inside. What do you see?

The correct answer is:
  "I see God's Love all around me".

The correct answer is:
  "I see God's Love within me"

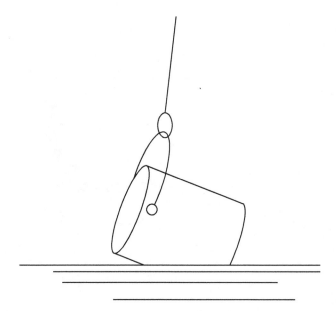

essence of prayer is intention, not attention

Ⓒ Resources for Reflection

The Spirit of Holiness

An Important parable

A Parable

Act of Consecration to the Holy Spirit

Prayer for the Seven Gifts of the Holy Spirit

Novena to the Holy Spirit (Especially for Pentecost)

Prayer is peaceful

the essence of prayer is intention, not attentio

1. Focus only on God often and as long as you can.

2. Moments of contemplation heal.

3. Contemplation is not mental; it is volitional.

4. From the cloud of forgetting step into the cloud of unknowing.

5. God alone is the source of true humility.

6. Only one thing is needed in prayer: loving God.

7. Contemplation is a simple intent, love reaching out to God.

8. "Holy Indifference" (Holy Acceptance) is the foundation of deep contemplation.

9. Passive contemplation is a free gift from God; it cannot be earned.

10. Contemplatives pray simply (Prayer of Simplicity).

Prayer soothes

essence of prayer is intention, not attention

11. Contemplation balances life. Prayer Soothes.

12. We must replace self-centeredness with God-centeredness for contemplation.

13. "Nothing" and "Nowhere" pertain to the senses, the physical realm.

14. Empty your mind of everything for a simple single focus on God as He is. Let God be Himself.

15. Keep your mind one with the One Who is Everything.

Prayer fulfills

the essence of prayer is intention, not attentio

16. Feed not your thoughts and feelings.

17. Contemplation is not "whating" God or self, but God be-ing and you be-ing together as one. The foundation of contemplation is not what you are, but God be-ing and you be-ing together as one.

18. Even the most ignorant person can experience union with God in perfect love by contemplating simply with humility.

19. What will most strengthen you? Best meet your needs? Most help you and others? Blind simple contemplation, because it opens you to God and His Blessings.

20. Contemplation leads to insights and true wisdom because it gives God your blindness and ignorance.

Prayer gives spiritual sight

e essence of prayer is intention, not attention

21. When you rest in the dark awareness of God as He is, He will vitalize and energize you.

22. Ours is not to know the how and why; ours is just to be in Darkness High.

23. The root, process, and fruit of contemplation is love: God's love and your love.

24. The analysis (understanding) of contemplation is not contemplation.

25. Contemplation is a union of love with God, which lessens self so Christ can increase.

Prayer focuses on God

the essence of prayer is intention, not attentio

26. Complete non-awareness of self
    leads to a complete awareness of God.

27. "Holy Indifference" accepts everything with peace.
    What is, is; what happens, happens.
    "Holy Acceptance".

28. Practicing contemplative prayer purifies
    and transforms the soul.

29. "Mystical union" means a direct immediate
    experience of God's Spirit to spirit, spirit in Spirit.

30. To intend God means to "stretch" towards God.

Prayer gives insight

essence of prayer is intention, not attention

31. Experiencing the "nothingness" and "no-whereness" of contemplation transforms a person.

32. Spiritual "knotting" is wrought in this "no-where" naught.

33. The discomfort of waiting for God in an unknown darkness leads to hope and comfort.

34. To pray in the darkness of faith means to be content with silence so that God can speak with the wordless words of the Word.

35. To pray in darkness is to be without light so that God can touch your soul with His sound-less Spirit.

Prayer intends God

the essence of prayer is intention, not attentio

36. In 16th c. St. Teresa of Jesus and St. John of the Cross taught mystical contemplation as mystical wisdom or mystical prayer.

    a. God's love for us is a dark flame.
    b. Secret wisdom means obscure, dark, formless knowledge (as described in "Cloud of Unknowing").

37. The Spiritual Canticle 39.12 "In contemplation God teaches the soul very quietly and secretly, without its knowing how, without the sound of words, and without the help of any bodily or spiritual faculty, in silence and quietude, in darkness to all sensory and natural things. Some spiritual persons call this contemplation knowing by unknowing." Our intellect and will are so intertwined in the soul that the experience to God's love necessarily leads to a kind of knowledge. God is known as unknown, as a mystery that we cannot know (the obscure night, the cloud of unknowing).

essence of prayer is intention, not attention

38. With our knowing power God is completely incomprehensible; with our loving power we can reach God.

39. Evagrius the Solitary (345 - 399 AD): "Pure prayer is no-thinking prayer."

40. St. Cassian of Imola (4th century: "Pure prayer is silent, imageless prayer of no thinking."

    St. Thomas: "The Gift of Wisdom from the Holy Spirit Who is Love poured into our hearts, is the source of contemplation."

Prayer equals union

the essence of prayer is intention, not attentio

41. Contemplation is silent love and union that leads to supra-conceptual wisdom. We are united with the One we do not know.

42. Contemplative union with Christ leads us into the Heart of the Holy Trinity.

43. Mystical theology is experiential knowledge of God through the embrace of unitive love.

44. God works "sine medio" in contemplation without the mediation of created things; Spirit to spirit without mediation.

45. St. John of the Cross: infused contemplation is "an inflow of God into the soul"; "a welling up of God in the soul".

"We love because He first loved us." 1 John. 4:19

> Mysticism is the wisdom that comes from loving. It has "nondiscriminating consciousness", only awareness, without subject or object.

*Prayer silences
our mind and heart*

e essence of prayer is intention, not attention

46. The 8 Beatitudes describe the non-differentiating consciousness of one who lives in the here and now with joy and without care. Mysticism is a journey through the ordinary. Mysticism is a process of becoming Christ-like and reliving His life and relationships.

Gal. 2:20 "It is no longer I who live but Christ Who lives in me." The mystical experience of Jesus Himself was primarily Trinitarian.

47. The call to contemplation is a journey from:

    a. Light to darkness

    b. Pasture to desert

    c. Many to nothing

A journey from:

    a. the familiar to the unfamiliar

    b. the known to the unknown

    c. the clear to the obscure

God is approached in darkness, emptiness, nothingness, the void.

the essence of prayer is intention, not attentio

48. Matt. 6:22-23 "The eye is the lamp of the body. So if your eye is sound, your whole body will be full of light; but if your eye is not sound our whole body will be full of darkness. If this light in you is darkness, how great the darkness."

49. Matt. 27:46 "My God, My God, why have You forsaken Me?" is from a profound experience of nothingness: no strength, no hope, total darkness, abandoned by God, without God's help, complete despair.

50. "This dark night (contemplation) is an inflow of God into the soul, which purges it of its habitual ignorance and imperfections."

Prayer finds God

essence of prayer is intention, not attention

51. Mystical Theology is an inflow of God into the soul to teach and perfect it with love. The Living Flame of Love is the Holy Spirit. "How gently and lovingly you wake in my heart." This awakening is a movement (activity) of the Word in the substance of the soul, and He contains the best of everything.

52. Secret love and secret wisdom — "secret" means beyond reasoning, thinking, clear and distinct ideas, incomprehensible. God is secret, a Hidden God, the Mystery of mysteries.

53. Being in love with God means loving without limits, qualifications, conditions, or reservations. God alone is Being-In-Love in the highest degree. Our being in love with God participates in His divine nature and we are divinized. This love is poured forth into our hearts by the Holy Spirit. This mystical love is the goal and climax of human living.

Prayer perfects

the essence of prayer is intention, not attentio

"Take, Lord, and receive
all my liberty, my memory,
my understanding, and my
entire will, All I have and
call my own.

You have given all to me.
To you, Lord, I return it.

Everything is yours; do with
it what you will. Give me
only your love and your grace,
that is enough for me.

Amen." St. Ignatius of Loyola

essence of prayer is intention, not attention

54. St. John of the Cross: "God is All in Himself, but nothing to us. Light in Himself, but darkness to us. Plenitude in Himself, but emptiness to us."

   a. Phil 2: "He emptied Himself" — in Japanese Bible "He made Himself nothing". Humility means being nothing.

   b. The kenotic God is the foundation of the kenotic Christ. The Father empties Himself of the Son, Who empties Himself of divine equality, divine position, divine privileges.

Spiritual Canticle 27:

"The tenderness and truth of love by which the immense Father favors and exalts this humble and loving soul reaches such a degree — 0 wonderful thing, worthy of all our awe and admiration! — that the Father himself becomes subject to her for her exaltation, as though he were her servant and she his Lord. And he is as solicitous in favoring her as he would be if he were her slave and she his God. So profound is the humility and sweetness of God."

the essence of prayer is intention, not attentio

Such is the loving kenosis of the Father. But to grasp the notion of emptiness in St John of the Cross it is necessary to say more. St. John of the Cross tells the contemplative to "desire to enter into Christ, into complete nudity, emptiness and poverty in everything in the world." This is the way of emptiness, the way of darkness, the way of nothing. It is the immortal todo y nada:

"To reach satisfaction in all
desire its possession in nothing.

To come to the knowledge of all
desire the knowledge of nothing.

To come to possess all
desire the possession of nothing.

To arrive at being all
desire to be nothing."

Prayer possess nothing

55. The Living Flame of Love is gentle and consoling, and then causes acute suffering of the dark night. Like fire, God absorbs the soul into Himself like a torrent of fire devouring a drop of water. This flame of love enkindles the will to love, desire, praise, thank and pray to God. The fiery dart of God's love wounds the heart and soul. Some become intoxicated by the Eucharistic Blood of Christ.

56. If we are emptied with Christ, we will be filled with Christ.

57. The circle is a symbol of God and a symbol of nothing; todo y nada; infinity and zero.

58. Pure faith, dark faith, naked faith, is aware of nothing. Infused contemplation is called a "ray of darkness".

Prayer is naked

the essence of prayer is intention, not attentio

59. St. John of the Cross: "Leave distinct particular knowledge for the vague, dark, general knowledge of pure, naked faith. Transcend rational knowledge to arrive at perfect wisdom." On his deathbed he said, "May the vision of thy beauty be my death." Song of Songs 5:2 "I slept, but my heart was awake." This means my senses, faculties, and powers were asleep, but my love was awake tending towards God.

Natural knowledge and scientific knowledge are perfected by Divine Wisdom and Divine Love.

Prayer is pure

essence of prayer is intention, not attention

60. "Theosis": Sharing in God's Beauty,
    Source of all beauty.

Spiritual Canticle 36:5

"That is: that I be so transformed in your beauty,
that we may be alike in beauty, and both behold
ourselves in your beauty, possessing then your very
beauty; this, in such a way that each looking at the
other may see in the other their own beauty, since
both are your beauty alone, I being absorbed in
your beauty; hence I shall see you in your beauty,
and you will see yourself in me in your beauty; that I
may resemble you in your beauty, and you resemble
me in your beauty, and my beauty be your beauty
and your beauty my beauty; wherefore I shall be you
in your beauty, and you will be me in your beauty,
because your very beauty will be my beauty; and
thus we shall behold each other in your beauty."

Prayer beautifies

the essence of prayer is intention, not attentio

essence of prayer is intention, not attention

Come, Holy Spirit, come!
And from your celestial home
Shed a ray of light divine!

Come, Father of the poor!
Come, source of all our store!
Come, within our bosoms shine.

You, of comforters the best;
You, the soul's most welcome guest;
Sweet refreshment here below;

In our labor, rest most sweet;
Grateful coolness in the heat;
Solace in the midst of woe.

O most blessed Light divine,
Shine within these hearts of thine,
And our inmost being fill!

the essence of prayer is intention, not attentio

Where you are not, we have naught,
Nothing good in deed or thought,
Nothing free from taint of ill.

Heal our wounds, our strength renew;
On our dryness pour your dew;
Wash the stains of guilt away;

Bend the stubborn heart and will;
Melt the frozen, warm the chill;
Guide the steps that go astray.

On the faithful, who adore
And confess you evermore
In your sevenfold gift descend;

Give them virtue's sure reward;
Give them your salvation, Lord;
Give them joys that never end.
Amen. Alleluia.

e essence of prayer is intention, not attention

The Spirit of Holiness

The best definition of holiness is being Christ-like in purity, humility, and charity. (Purity means having a clear heart as Jesus has.) The Holy Spirit is the Spirit of Holiness because He is the Spirit of Christ; that is, the One Who made Christ Who He is. Everything the Holy Spirit did for Jesus from His conception to His Ascension into heaven, the Holy Spirit wants to do for us, IF we will allow Him and cooperate with Him. This is why developing a deep devotion to the Holy Spirit is so important for Christians.

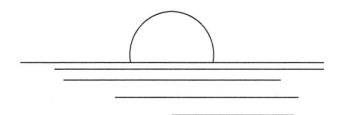

the essence of prayer is intention, not attentia

An Important Parable

If God were to grant you one wish, what would you wish for. (You cannot wish for many wishes.) The wish has to be personal for yourself – you cannot wish for peace in the world.

You cannot wish for heaven, because according to Scripture heaven has to be earned. The best analogy for heaven is someone paddling upstream in a canoe. If he stops paddling, he will drift backwards and may go over the waterfall.

A connection with marriage: the best analogy for marriage is husband and wife paddling upstream in a canoe. If one stops paddling, the other has to work harder to keep the marriage going. If both stops paddling, the canoe will drift backwards until it goes over the waterfall and break up on the rocks. The moral is: do not marry an armless person; that is, someone who will not work on the marriage or is unable to work on the marriage.

essence of prayer is intention, not attention

A Parable

A poor peasant lived on a small plot of land with his wife and parents in a small cottage. He would cut firewood in the forest to sell at the nearby villages. One day an angel appeared to him in the forest and said, "God will give you one wish. Return in a week to state your wish and God will grant it."

He rushes home to tell the good news. That night his father tells him, "Son, I'm your father. You know how much your mother and I have wanted a piece of land with a cottage of our own. Then you and your wife will have the privacy you want."

The next morning, his mother tells him, "Son, I'm your mother; you know what a burden I've been since I went blind five years ago. Ask God to restore my sight. Then I can help in the garden and inside."

That evening his wife tells him, "I'm your wife. We've been married 12 years, and you know how much we have wanted a child. And a child would bring such joy to your parents. Ask God to grant us a child."

the essence of prayer is intention, not attentic

He doesn't know what to do. He doesn't want to disappoint or hurt any of his loved ones. So he seeks out a holy monk at the monastery to ask his advice.

The monk tells him, "I will fast and spend the night in prayer to seek the guidance of the Holy Spirit. Come back tomorrow morning to receive this guidance from the Holy Spirit. He returns the next morning to receive this guidance.

When the angel appears to him in the forest to ask for his one wish, he says, "My wish is that 22 months from today, my mother will be watching my son drink out of a solid gold cup encrusted with gems."

His all-in-one wish brought joy to everyone. My all-in-one wish is for the fullness of the Holy Spirit with the fullness of His Gifts

essence of prayer is intention, not attention

Act of Consecration to the Holy Spirit

Holy Spirit, Divine Spirit of Light and Love, I consecrate to my mind, heart and will. May my understanding be always submissive to Your inspirations. Inflame my heart with love for God and for others. Conform my will to the Divine Will, and help me to relive the virtues and life of Jesus: His purity, humility, and charity; to Whom with the Father, and You be glory forever.

Amen.

the essence of prayer is intention, not attenti

Prayer for the Seven Gifts of the Holy Spirit

Christ Jesus, before ascending into heaven, You promised to send the Holy Spirit to Your apostles and disciples. Grant that the same Spirit may perfect in our lives the work of Your grace and love. Grant us the Spirit of Fear of the Lord that we may be filled with a loving reverence toward You. the Spirit of Piety that we may find peace and fulfillment in the service of God while serving others; the Spirit of Fortitude that we may bear our cross with You and, with courage, overcome the obstacles that interfere with our salvation; the Spirit of Knowledge that we may know You and know ourselves and grow in holiness; the Spirit of Understanding to enlighten our minds with the light of Your truth; the Spirit of Counsel that we may choose the surest way of doing Your will, seeking first the Kingdom; Grant us the Spirit of Wisdom that we may aspire to the things that last forever; Teach us to be Your faithful disciples and animate us in every way with Your Spirit.

Amen.

essence of prayer is intention, not attention

Novena to the Holy Spirit (Especially for Pentecost)

FIRST DAY - Creation Awaits Fulfillment

Holy Spirit, Lord of light! From Your clear celestial height, Your pure beaming radiance give! Almighty and eternal God, send forth Your Spirit, who brought order from chaos at the beginning of the universe, and peace to the Lord's disciples. Grant that I, as your creation, baptized in your Spirit, may be filled with the seven gifts so that I may forever do your will and renew the face of the earth.

Amen.

Pray: Our Father, Hail Mary & Glory be

Pray: Act of Consecration to the Holy Spirit & Prayer for the Seven Gifts of the Holy Spirit

SECOND DAY - Christ's Promise to
Send the Paraclete

Come, Father of the poor! Come, treasures which
endure! Come, Light of all that live! Come, O
Blessed Spirit of Holy Fear, fill me with devotion
to God alone. In the Risen Christ, I welcome You,
O Spirit of truth, whom the Father sends in Jesus'
name. Wash clean the sinful soul, and rain down
your grace that we may be one with the Church in
fidelity to our Lord Jesus, Christ.

Amen.

Pray: Our Father, Hail Mary & Glory be

Pray: Act of Consecration to the Holy Spirit &
Prayer for the Seven Gifts of the Holy Spirit

essence of prayer is intention, not attention

THIRD DAY - The Soul of Christ's
Body, The Church

Thou, of all consolers, best, Visiting the troubled breast dost refreshing peace bestow. Come, O Blessed Spirit of Piety, possess my heart. God, our Father, may I, through the grace of your Spirit, be forever filled with filial affection for you. Grant that I may be inspired to love and respect all members of your family as brothers and sisters of Jesus, who, together with him, call you Abba, Father.

Amen.

Pray: Our Father, Hail Mary & Glory be

Pray: Act of Consecration to the Holy Spirit & Prayer for the Seven Gifts of the Holy Spirit

the essence of prayer is intention, not attentia

FOURTH DAY - The Dignity of the Christian

Thou, in toil art comfort sweet; Pleasant coolness in the heat; Solace in the midst of woe. Come, O Blessed Spirit of Fortitude, uphold my soul in time of trouble and adversity. O, Divine Trinity, grant that we may be strengthened to see in ourselves and each other the dignity that is ours as temples of Your Holy Spirit, to be loved by one another as each of us is loved by Jesus. We ask this through Christ, our Lord.

Amen.

Pray: Our Father, Hail Mary & Glory be

Pray: Act of Consecration to the Holy Spirit & Prayer for the Seven Gifts of the Holy Spirit

essence of prayer is intention, not attention

FIFTH DAY - Gifted to Serve and Build Others Up

Light immortal! Light Divine! Visit Thou these hearts of Thine, and our inmost being fill! Come, 0 Blessed Spirit of Knowledge, and grant that I may perceive the will of the Father. Father, through Your Spirit, You invite us to participate in the fullness of Creation. Help me to see that all gifts are from You and intended for your Glory. For there are many different gifts, but always the same Spirit, many ways of serving, but 'always the same Lord.

Amen. Pray: Our Father, Hail Mary & Glory be

Pray: Act of Consecration to the Holy Spirit & Prayer for The Seven Gifts of the Holy Spirit

the essence of prayer is intention, not attenti

FOURTH DAY - The Dignity of the Christian

Thou, in toil art comfort sweet; Pleasant coolness in the heat; Solace in the midst of woe. Come, O Blessed Spirit of Fortitude, uphold my soul in time of trouble and adversity. O, Divine Trinity, grant that we may be strengthened to see in ourselves and each other the dignity that is ours as temples of Your Holy Spirit, to be loved by one another as each of us is loved by Jesus. We ask this through Christ, our Lord.

Amen.

Pray: Our Father, Hail Mary & Glory be

Pray: Act of Consecration to the Holy Spirit & Prayer for the Seven Gifts of the Holy Spirit

essence of prayer is intention, not attention

SIXTH DAY - Human Weakness and Sinfulness

If Thou take Thy grace away, nothing pure in man will stay, All his good is turned to ill. Come, 0 Blessed Spirit of Understanding, enlighten our minds so that we may appreciate and see more fully what we know by faith. Come to us in our weakness and give voice to our petitions, for "the prayers that the Spirit makes for God's holy people are always in accordance with the mind of God."

Amen.

Pray: Our Father, Hail Mary & Glory be

Pray: Act of Consecration to the Holy Spirit & Prayer for The Seven Gifts of the Holy Spirit

the essence of prayer is intention, not attentio

SEVENTH DAY - Growth in the Freedom
that Love Gives

Heal our wounds - our strength renew; On our dryness, pour thy dew; Wash the stains of guilt away! Come, 0 Blessed Spirit of Counsel. Make my thoughts holy, my love pure, and my works pleasing to God. Father, guided by Your Spirit, may I strive to make loving choices and respect all life. May we be aware of our dignity as Your sons and daughters, redeemed with the Blood of Your beloved Son, Jesus Christ, Our Lord.

Amen.

Pray: Our Father, Hail Mary & Glory be

Pray: Act of Consecration to the Holy Spirit & Prayer for The Seven Gifts of the Holy Spirit

essence of prayer is intention, not attention

EIGHTH DAY - Gifted through the Spirit

Bend the stubborn heart and will; Melt the frozen, warm the chill; Guide the steps that go astray! Come, 0 Blessed Spirit of Wisdom, strengthen my faith, increase my hope, perfect my charity. Father, enlighten us each day, in the silence of our hearts, to discern the voice of Your Spirit, to do what He asks of us and to understand the gifts He freely gives us. We ask this through Christ our Lord.

Amen.

Pray: Our Father, Hail Mary & Glory be

Pray: Act of Consecration to the Holy Spirit & Prayer for he Seven Gifts of the Holy Spirit

the essence of prayer is intention, not attentio

NINTH DAY - Sent with the Power to Reconcile

Thou on those who evermore, Thee confess and Thee adore, In Thy sevenfold gifts, descend; Give them comfort when they die; Give them life with Thee on high; Give them joys which never end. Amen. Father, through Jesus, Your Son, You sent the Paraclete to be at our side, to reconcile all Creation to you. Grant that I may be forever open to Jesus' invitation to "Receive The Holy Spirit!" Father, open our hearts to accept Your forgiveness for our sins and to offer that same forgiveness to those who we feel have offended us. For merciful forgiveness is the essence of Your love revealed in Your Son. Come, O Divine Spirit, fill my heart with Your Heavenly Fruits - Your charity, joy, peace patience, benignity, goodness, faith, mildness and temperance, that I may, by faithful submission to your Inspiration, merit to be united eternally with You in the love of the Father and the Son.

Amen.

Pray: Our Father, Hail Mary & Glory be

Pray: Act of Consecration to the Holy Spirit & Prayer for The Seven Gifts of the Holy Spirit

essence of prayer is intention, not attention

No desire
No knowledge
No light
No place
No time
No why
Only darkness
In this nowhere darkness
Timeless darkness
Empty darkness
Is born the Son
Light of the world
One with the Father
In the Love of the Holy Spirit
This ongoing birth of the Son
within you
makes you
one with the Father
in the Love of the Holy Spirit ·······························

the essence of prayer is intention, not attentic

to radiate peace to others

Conclusion

The absence of activity in contemplative prayer is only apparent. Below the surface, the mind and will are drawn into the orbit of an activity that is deep and intense and supernatural, and which overflows into our whole being and brings forth incalculable fruits.

There is no such thing a kind of prayer in which you do absolutely nothing. If you are doing nothing you are not praying. On the other hand, if God is the source of your interior activity, the work or your faculties may be entirely beyond conscious estimation, and its results may to be seen or understood.

Contemplative prayer is a deep and simplified spiritual activity in which the mind and will rest in a unified and simple concentration upon God, turned to Him, intent upon Him and absorbed in His own light, with a simple gaze which is perfect adoration because it silently tells God that we have left everything else and desire even to leave our own selves for His sake, and that He alone is important to us, He alone is our desire and our life, and nothing else can give us any joy.

What you most need in this dark journey is an unfaltering trust in the Divine guidance, as well as the courage to risk everything for Him.

Thomas Merton.

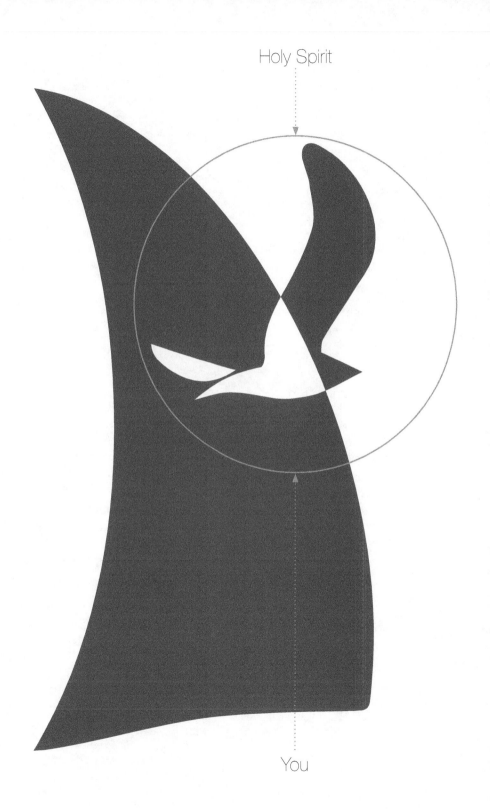

Holy Spirit

You

Index

A

Abbot John Chapman
31, 97-106

Answers (Quiz)
19, 21, 23, 25

APT Living
174

C

Contemplation
12, 134-136, 196-197

D

Devotional
12

Distractions
61

E

Emotions
52-56, 91

F

Flexibility
28

Foes
91

Forgiveness
87, 89, 90

G

Grudges
86-87

H

Heart of Prayerfulness
158

Helen Malecoat – "I AM"
68

Holy Acceptance
104, 197, 201

Holy Spirit

Consecration to -
75, 223
Gifts of - 126
Novena to - 223 - 233
Spirit of Holiness -
218
Spirit of Prayer - 66

I

Immediacy
28-29

Inner Peace
48-49

J

Jesus Prayer
109, 111, 138, 140

John Chapman, Abbot
  31, 97-106

L

Lectio Divina
  115-118

Liturgical Prayer
  9, 12, 14, 135

Liturgy
  9, 16

O

Oneness
  28

P

Prayer
  Benefits of - 4, 65
  For the Seven Gifts
  of the Holy Spirit -
  222

Prayer of
  St. Francis of Assisi -
  124, 178

  St. Ignatius of Loyola
  209

Prayer to
  Holy Spirit -
  147, 182

Q

Questions (Quiz)
  18, 20, 22, 24

S

Serenity Prayers
  76-77

Silent Contemplation
  160

St. Anthony the Great
  8

St. Damien of Molokai
  113

St. Teresa of Avila
  37, 184

St. Teresa of Calcutta
  4

T

Thomas Merton
  236

Sailing with God

Fr. Chun uses the simple and beautiful imagery of "Sailing with God," a very useful and practical way to enter into the dimensions of mental prayer. Drawing upon our rich Catholic spiritual tradition, along with his many years of experience as a teacher and spiritual director, he shows us how to set out on the sea of prayer, pushed along by the breath of the Holy Spirit.

It is my hope that many will pick up this simple book and learn how to pray in a way that has, up till now, seemed out of reach for some. May the reader be blessed as he or she discovers whole new horizons in their prayerful communion with our loving and merciful God. He is calling you. It is part of the universal call to holiness that is ours by virtue of our baptism. May you answer the call to prayer.

From the Foreward of Archbishop Alexander Sample of Portland, Oregon,

"Using this book and absorbing its insights will transform your entire understanding of prayer, and elevate your attitude towards prayer."

Fr. Francis Chun, S.T.L.

Born and raised as a Buddhist in Honolulu, Hawaii, the author became a Catholic at age 14. After receiving his B.A. in Philosophy and Theology, he taught Religious Studies in high school in San Francisco for 3 years before earning his Licentiate in Sacred Theology after 4 years of study under the Dominicans at the University of Fribourg in Switzerland. As a Catholic priest for 55 years, he has taught Theology in high school and in college, and gives retreats and workshops to Religious and parishes.

ISBN 9780578412061

9 0 0 0 0 >

ISBN 9780578412061

U.S. $20
Paschal Peace Press
paschalpeacepress@gmail.co

"Singing a prayer is worth two prayers"

CPSIA information can be obtained
at www.ICGtesting.com
Printed in the USA
FFHW010821291118
49698170-54098FF